"This book is a gem. In an articulate and lucid manner, Roshi Shishin Wick opens up one of the most difficult aspects of spiritual experience: the complete identity and ceaseless interplay of the relative—the truth of each unique moment and individual life, of separateness and irreplaceability—with the absolute—the never-divided oneness of all that everlastingly *is*."

—ROSHI JAN CHOZEN BAYS, abbot of Great Vow Zen Monastery

"At the very summit of Zen training are the Five Ranks of Tozan. These are usually examined only at the very end of koan study because they are the ultimate challenge: the final barrier. I am grateful to Shishin Roshi for such an accessible analysis of this profound teaching."

—DAVID R. LOY, author of *Nonduality: In Buddhism and Beyond*

"If you want to know the heart of Zen, here you are! This book is a wonderful and wise companion for anyone walking the intimate way. Gerry Shishin Wick walks us through Tozan's five ranks, points us faithfully toward the deeper invitation, and guides us as we make our own way. This is a guide book for spiritual life. It reveals the intimate way as mysterious and beautiful and right in front of us. This belongs in the library of anyone who wants to understand Zen. And, more, it should be read. And then read again. A wonderful book."

—JAMES ISHMAEL FORD, author of *The Intimate Way of Zen: Effort, Surrender, and Awakening on the Spiritual Journey*

"My Dharma brother Shishin offers up this sparkling, faceted jewel after decades of Zen study and training. In the true spirit of Master Tozan's Five Ranks, his exposition is at once direct and expansive, conceptual and intimate, vital and mysterious. Please accept this open-handed invitation and sink deeply into the mystery."

—ROSHI WENDY EGYOKU NAKAO, Abbot Emerita, Zen Center of Los Angeles

THE FIVE RANKS OF ZEN

Tozan's Path of Being, Nonbeing, and Compassion

GERRY SHISHIN WICK

FOREWORD BY NORMAN FISCHER

SHAMBHALA

Shambhala Publications, Inc.
2129 13th Street
Boulder, Colorado 80302
www.shambhala.com

Cover art: "A Long Way Down" by Kim Knoll
Cover design: Daniel Urban-Brown
Interior design: Katrina Noble

9 8 7 6 5 4 3 2 1

First Edition
Printed in the United States of America

Shambhala Publications makes every effort to print on acid-free, recycled paper.
Shambhala Publications is distributed worldwide by Penguin Random House, Inc., and its subsidiaries.

LIBRARY OF CONGRESS CATALOGING-IN-PUBLICATION DATA
Names: Wick, Gerry Shishin, author.
Title: The five ranks of Zen: Tozan's path of being, nonbeing, and compassion / Gerry Shishin Wick; foreword by Norman Fischer.
Description: Boulder: Shambhala Publications, 2024. |
Includes bibliographical references and index. |
Identifiers: LCCN 2023052886 | ISBN 9781645473220
(trade paperback)
Subjects: LCSH: Spiritual life—Zen Buddhism. | Truth—Religious aspects—Buddhism. | Zen Buddhism—Doctrines.
Classification: LCC BQ9288 .W53 2024 | DDC 294.3/444—dc23/
eng/20240109
LC record available at https://lccn.loc.gov/2023052886

Dedicated to Roshi Bernie Glassman, my brother,
my mentor, my friend, and a true mensch

CONTENTS

FOREWORD

ZEN PRACTICE is experiential, rough, improvisational, and avowedly hostile to all forms of doctrine. "Directly pointing to the mind," as Bodhidharma, the legendary Zen founder, says.

And yet the truth is, profound Mahayana Buddhist teachings inform it. To someone who knows these teachings, Zen dialogues are marvelously pithy expressions of the most important Mahayana ideas, from the insights of the emptiness teachings, to the Mind Only School's deepest contemplations, to the ever-shifting facets of Hwa Yen's jewel-like discourse.

Why, then, is Zen literature so spare? And why does it so strenuously resist explanation?

It's because the fundamental Zen impulse (perhaps a Chinese reaction to an over-complicated Indian tradition) is to cut through to the core, to present essential Buddhism concretely, not as an elaborate way of thinking but as lived experience.

And yet, despite this, there are some Zen teachings that do systematize and explain without, somehow, violating Zen's dynamic directness. Perhaps chief among such teachings is Tozan's famous Five Ranks.

I have always been fascinated with the Five Ranks, and have often studied them on my own, but without much success. While I had some intuitive appreciation of them, I had a hard time decoding the details. So I have generally left them alone and almost never speak about them in Dharma talks. (I have justified this omission with the rumor that Dogen, the founder of the Soto school of Zen that Shishin and I practice, didn't like the Five Ranks and considered them needlessly complicated.)

But those days are gone, because I—and you—now have, as far as I know, the first clear, practice-based explication of Tozan's Five Ranks for the Western Zen student! I am really glad to finally be able to hear clearly what Tozan has been patiently trying to tell me.

Gerry Shishin Wick is a solid Zen teacher of many years' experience. While we have only briefly met, I have long admired his useful commentary to *The Book of Equanimity*, an important collection of one hundred Zen koans, and I go to it frequently when I am studying and lecturing from that text. He has a way of making cogent what seems perplexing, without ever diluting the depths of the teachings or robbing the reader of the necessary work that makes understanding truly worthwhile.

He has done this same job for the Five Ranks.

Zen practice is the work of a lifetime and beyond because there is no end to the deepening of wisdom and compassion. And yet there are phases, steps and stages, triumphs and defeats, pitfalls and pratfalls, along the way—which is what the Five Ranks are about: how a lifetime of practice unfolds, and how the puzzle pieces of the various insights and misunderstandings that arise fit together.

While what I have just said is true, it is also misleading, since Zen practice is essentially circuitous, all-inclusive, and impossible to codify. In the end there is really nothing to know, nothing to acquire, and, in a profound sense, no development at all. The Five Ranks teaching takes this into account—and Shishin understands it very well.

As a person who has practiced Zen for more than sixty years and studied closely for decades under Hakuyu Taizan Maezumi, a thorough-going and foundational Japanese Zen master, Shishin knows the Five Ranks as well as anyone. Here he shares compassionately and generously the fruit of his long and close instruction with the roshi, as well as his own experience. As a deeply experienced Zen teacher, he knows the challenges the contemporary practitioner faces, as well as the transformative possibilities.

The Five Ranks of Zen is a patient and a systematic text. At the same time, there is an ease and a humility you will sense as you read, as if the author loves the teachings he is transmitting, sees them broadly and with facility, and really wants to share them with you, person to person. I especially appreciated Shishin's many references to Zen and other Buddhist stories and teachings—placing them within the explanatory construct of the Ranks.

I feel grateful to have this book. And honored to have been asked to introduce it to you. If you are a Zen practitioner of some experience, you will appreciate it as I do, as if an eloquent and heartfelt personal letter from an old friend about an urgent matter of concern to you both—and you will find yourself going back to it again and again. If you are new to Zen, you will appreciate having a clear and realistic map to orient you to what lies ahead.

Either way, Shishin's exposition of Tozan's Five Ranks will be a sturdy and helpful companion for the journey.

—NORMAN FISCHER

PREFACE

W HEN I STUDIED the Five Ranks of Tozan with my teacher, Taizan Maezumi Roshi, it was the culmination of my twelve years of koan study with him. We met almost daily in the *dokusan* (private interview) room at the Zen Center of Los Angeles. In those sessions, Maezumi Roshi pushed and prodded me to clarify my understanding of the Five Ranks. I had to express that understanding to him using live words based on the insights that occurred during my meditation. In Zen parlance, "dead words" are conceptual and intellectual, while "live words" come from penetrating into the profound meanings of the Five Ranks using the wisdom of the entire body. Maezumi Roshi was an expert at drawing out the wisdom of his students. It was in the dokusan room where he was at his best.

Maezumi Roshi had a unique background in Zen. He grew up in a Soto Zen family temple where his father, Baian Hakujun Kuroda, was his first Zen teacher. During college, he lived and studied with Koryu Osaka Roshi, who was a lay Rinzai master. In Los Angeles, he met Hakuun Yasutani Roshi, who, with his teacher Harada Daiun Sogaku Roshi, combined Soto and Rinzai teachings. Maezumi Roshi became a Dharma successor of all three of his teachers and thus was well trained in the Soto and Rinzai traditions. He imparted that understanding to his successors. In 1990, he empowered me as an independent Zen teacher.

Maezumi Roshi immigrated to the United States from Japan in 1956 to function as a Soto Zen priest at Zenshuji, the Japanese Buddhist temple in the Little Tokyo district of Los Angeles. In 1965, he founded the Zen Center of Los Angeles to bring the teachings of Zen to Westerners. We met in 1972, and I spent twenty-three years studying with him until his death in 1995.

Since Master Tozan was a founder of the Soto school, his teachings are studied in Soto Zen Centers and temples around the world. The Five Ranks of Tozan are included in the koan curriculum of all the major Rinzai lineages. Thus, the Five Ranks are universally revered in the Zen world. Zen practitioners of all stripes are exposed to Tozan and his Five Ranks.

From my study of the ranks with Maezumi Roshi, I was able to unify and consolidate all of my Zen training with him. Among the many things I learned, two lessons stand out. The first is the intimate relationship between the relative reality and the absolute reality. The Hindu greeting "Namaste" demonstrates this relationship. I see the term as more than a casual greeting between friends. When I press the palms of my hands together in reverence, it unifies all opposites. There is no separation between self and others. Then, speaking the word *Namaste* invokes the sacred within the profane. For me, *Namaste* means that the divine in me bows to and recognizes the divine in you. This simple gesture reminds me that everyone and everything is sacred and divine and, at the same time, ordinary and profane. That is one teaching of the Five Ranks of Tozan.

The second lesson is to surrender to the unknown and let go of our attachments, cherished opinions, and habit-ridden consciousness. Through my many years of Zen practice, I've learned that I have gained nothing and have accumulated nothing. But I have let go of many things. Tozan emphasizes that point over and over again. There is no need to laud any accomplishments in Zen. Overconfidence and the pride of accomplishment serve no useful purpose. It is better to keep letting them go while progressing on the path of the Buddha.

Life is a mystery. We don't know what will happen in the next moment. We don't know whether we will be dead or alive. Learning to maintain equanimity in the midst of the unknown is one of the greatest lessons of Zen. Master Tozan emphasizes that lesson.

o   o   o   o   o

In the course of writing this book, I reviewed several translations of the Five Ranks. At the beginning of each of my commentaries on the individual ranks, I have included three or four translations to show the range of presentations.

However, in the subsequent interpretations I give in each chapter, I focus primarily on the translations I used in my studies of the Five Ranks with Maezumi Roshi.

In this book I make many references to Zen koans and to the writings of Dogen, particularly his major works, *Shobogenzo* and *Eihei Koroku*. Rather than clutter the book with numerous endnotes, for koans I will make a reference to the koan collection and the case number in the main text. For Dogen's writings, I will reference the fascicle (chapter) name and the volume in which it appears. I also will not use endnotes for some famous Zen verses, including *The Song of the Jewel Mirror Samadhi* (*Hokyozanmai*), *The Identity of Relative and Absolute* (*Sandokai*), and *Trust in Heart/Mind* (*Xinxin Ming*).

The four major books of koan collections that I reference most often are listed here (with Japanese names in parentheses). I will use their English names in this text. In the White Plum lineage, we also study one hundred to two hundred koans that are drawn from a variety of sources, including *Entangling Vines*.[1] Most of them are not in any standard koan collections. I will refer to them as "miscellaneous koans" in this text.

> *The Gateless Gate* (*Mumonkan*)
> *The Blue Cliff Record* (*Hekiganroku*)
> *The Book of Equanimity* (*Shoyuroku*)
> *The Transmission of Light* (*Denkoroku*)

To see the main translations of koan collections, works by Dogen, Zen verses, and other Chan and Zen classics that

I consulted in writing this book, please see the selected bibliography.

With few exceptions, I use the Japanese names for the Chinese Zen ancestors. When I studied with Maezumi Roshi, he used the Japanese names, and those are the transliterations with which I am familiar. There is a tendency to use the Chinese spelling these days, and I offer them parenthetically when first mentioning a new name or term, but I have to admit that I know Tozan, but I do not know Dongshan. With apologies to Chinese speakers, I am just too old and stubborn to change. One exception is the Sixth Chinese Ancestor. His Chinese name, Huineng, is better known than his Japanese name, Eno.

o   o   o   o   o

In addition to bringing the subtle teachings of Tozan's Five Ranks to a wider audience, one of my intentions in writing this book is to create a reference book for the systematic study of the Five Ranks as koans in the Zen tradition. It is probably natural that you will want to first read through the entire book to get an overview of what the Five Ranks are offering so that you sense the overall shape of the teachings.

After getting an overview, to really work with the Five Ranks as a practitioner, you would need to sit with just one line of each rank at a time. It's too rich a meal to rush through. You need to sink into it. And hopefully you will regularly want to refer back to this book as you journey on the path of the Buddha.

ACKNOWLEDGMENTS

THE BOOK HAS had a long gestation period. About twenty years ago, I felt that Tozan's Five Ranks needed to be made more accessible to followers of Zen Buddhism. I was not sure how to do that, and I let the idea percolate on a back burner in my mind. Then about ten years ago, I asked Bernie Glassman if he wanted to join me on this venture, and he agreed. We met several times at his home in Montague, Massachusetts, and discussed how to approach the Five Ranks. I recorded our conversations and transcribed the most relevant parts. Unfortunately, Bernie had a stroke and died a few years later.

The book floundered for a few more years until I forced the issue by giving talks to my sangha at the Great Mountain Zen Center in Berthoud, Colorado. But the beginnings of the book really started to take shape when Koshin Paley Ellison, Robert Chodo Campbell, and Mahyar Hassid of the New York Zen Center for Contemplative Care asked me to teach a course during one of their training periods. I used Tozan's Five Ranks as the basis of the course, and I was able to produce a crude draft of the book from my notes. I give my thanks to Koshin, Chodo, Mahyar, and those who attended my talks, both in Colorado and in New York, for their feedback and questions.

I am especially grateful to Matt Zepelin of Shambhala Publications, whose keen insight and holistic view brought clarity to the manuscript. Sean Tetsudo Murphy pored over the original manuscript and made many suggestions and additions that helped shape the initial blob. Wendy Egyoku Nakao and Bobby Chowa Werner read an early version and gave me much constructive feedback. Others who contributed insights, corrections, and suggestions include Tania Casselle, Paul Gyodo Agostinelli, and Karin Kempe. I am also grateful to Breanna Locke, Karen Steib, and the other editors at Shambhala Publications for seeing the book through to completion. Zoketsu Norman Fischer graciously contributed an insightful foreword that helps to set the scene. My wife, Ilia Shinko Perez, supported me through this process. Many thanks to all.

I am eternally grateful to Taizan Maezumi Roshi for introducing me to Tozan's Five Ranks and guiding me through their subtle meanings in private meetings in the dokusan room. I am also indebted to Bernie Glassman, who made himself available to discuss Tozan's intent and to provide his own unique perspective.

I only hope that my objective of bringing the teaching of Tozan to a wider audience is realized in this book. All omissions and errors are, of course, solely my responsibility.

PART ONE

THE FIVE
RANKS OF ZEN

THE FIVE RANKS OF TOZAN are the pinnacle of
Zen practice. Their subtle meaning serves as the
adhesive that bonds together all the teachings of
our Zen ancestors. In parts two and three of this
book, we will look in detail at two sets of five ranks
and how to integrate them into our Zen practice.
Part two contains the Hensho Goi, which examine
the relationship between the relative and absolute
realities. These ranks, or *goi*, are the most familiar
to Zen practitioners. In part three we will explore
the Kokun Goi, which focus on lineal stages of
the Zen path from the beginning practice to full
enlightenment.

This first part of the book looks at general characteristics of the Five Ranks and considers how the
relative and the absolute appear in our lives. It also
talks about the life of Master Tozan.

1

Aspects of the Five Ranks

How priceless is the merit gained through the step-by-step practice of the Five Ranks of the Absolute and the Relative!

—ZEN MASTER HAKUIN (1686–1769)

THE FIVE RANKS OF ZEN were first elucidated by the ninth-century Zen master Tozan (Ch. Dongshan Liangjie) and have become essential in the training of Zen students from all lineages. In my lineage, the White Plum lineage founded by the venerable Taizan Maezumi Roshi, the Five Ranks are studied at the end of our koan curriculum as the pinnacle of our training. In a way, they are also a summary of all the koan study that preceded them. My Dharma sister Roshi Egyoku Nakao told me that when her senior students start to study the Five Ranks, many of them have an "aha" moment when everything falls into place.

When I studied physics at Pomona College, we were taught different subjects—such as mechanics, optics, electricity and magnetism, thermodynamics, and atomic physics—as if they were separate and self-contained. Then, as I dug deeper into the material in graduate school at the University of California, Berkeley, it became obvious that each subject overlapped and interacted with every other subject. For example, the study of thermodynamics informed the study of mechanics. That, in turn, informed electricity and magnetism, which informed atomic physics, which also was informed by thermodynamics, and so forth. Physicists continue to seek a unifying theory that includes everything. In an analogous way, the Five Ranks are the unifying theory of Zen.

The marvelous secrets contained within the Five Ranks, however, will not be revealed through conceptual study. In order to understand the Five Ranks, you must experience them with your entire body, not just with the cells of your brain. They must penetrate your heart, bones, and marrow for the depths of their content to be revealed.

Most commentaries and books about the Five Ranks take a didactic or scholarly approach or try to explain Tozan's teachings. In this book, I will introduce the Five Ranks in a conceptual way but emphasize their significance for our daily lives. If they do not impact our lives, they become artificial and sterile and are worthless as Zen teachings.

The Five Ranks represent different ways of experiencing the relationship between and interpenetration of the absolute and relative spheres of reality. From the relative perspective, each of us manifests reality in a human form with all of our relationships, foibles, and brilliance. From the absolute perspective, each of us is whole, complete, spacious, transparent, and luminous. I suspect all of us can relate to the relative aspect of being human, yet we don't always experience ourselves as having qualities such as completeness and luminosity. Perhaps this book will assist you in transforming your understanding of the relative and recognizing your existence within the absolute.

o   o   o   o   o

What does the term "Five Ranks" actually mean? Some Zen teachers prefer to use words other than *rank* to describe this teaching. Robert Aitken Roshi uses *modes*; Roshi Egyoku Nakao uses the word *positions*. Their concern is that *rank* implies a progression, whereas the Zen view is that no step is better than the others since the entirety of the teaching is contained in each step. Zen would agree with William Blake's exhortation "to see a world in a grain of sand and a heaven in a wildflower."[1] I'll stick with *ranks* in this book, however, because most translators use that word, and it is the word used by Maezumi Roshi.

As you've likely noticed, the Five Ranks are in reference to something—the relative and the absolute. When I first heard the words *relative* and *absolute*, I found it difficult to connect them to my ordinary life. They seemed so abstract. It took some learning about the conceptual development and practices of Buddhism for me to begin to contextualize these terms in an experiential way.

The initial teachings of Buddhism emphasized the importance of emptiness, or the absolute basis of reality. Emptiness implies that everything is impermanent and has no fixed qualities. This includes the notion of a fixed, abiding self that most of us cling to. Our self is empty. This emptiness is the absolute because everything, without exception, is empty of a fixed nature. When I had glimpses of the absolute, it helped me understand that "my problems" were small wrinkles in space and time, and that these problems were not even "mine." It enabled me to see the futility of clinging to my dramas and freed me to a large degree from the suffering that I carried.

The absolute is also identified with the experience of unity or oneness. In this absolute state, there is no self and no other, thus everything is one.

Later Buddhist teachings pointed out the fallacy of emphasizing the absolute at the expense of the relative. The Perfection of Wisdom Sutra (Prajna Paramita Sutra), written about 100 B.C.E., exemplifies this approach in its denial of the duality of nirvana and samsara (the realm of our everyday lives, seen as a realm filled with much suffering).

One Zen koan reduces this view to its pithiest form by saying, "Samsara is nirvana." How do you understand that?

A Zen master once said to his student, "You're always complaining about having so many problems. I know a place where there are at least ten thousand people, and not one of them has even a single problem or worry. Would you like me to take you there?"

His student said, "Yes, please do!"

The master took him to a cemetery. As they looked out upon the collection of graves and headstones, the master exclaimed, "Die while alive, and then you can be free no matter what arises in your life!"

The student had a sudden realization and stopped complaining. He still had problems, but he looked at them in a different way. The student understood the master's instruction to let his ego-grasping mind die. He had been shocked into awakening, and he could now see the illusory nature of his problems.

The Buddha taught that suffering is inherent in life. He also taught that there is a cause for suffering and a means to transform suffering into contentment. That transformation requires seeing the true nature of things.

The great Buddhist philosopher Nagarjuna lived in the first and second centuries in India. One of the major figures of Mahayana Buddhism, he is also considered one of the most deeply accomplished masters in our Zen lineage. Nagarjuna put Buddhist experience into a philosophical system called Madhyamaka, which espouses the Middle Way. He asserted that everything we believe exists and has permanence exists by virtue of its opposite, and thus it is subject to change and impermanence.

Let's make this more concrete with a few simple examples. According to Nagarjuna, each side is defined by the other side. *Yes* makes no sense without *no* to compare it with. *Up* makes no sense without its opposite, *down*, and so forth.

Therefore, each side is inseparable and interdependent. It follows that nirvana and samsara constitute one inseparable reality. Nagarjuna concluded that all dharmas (phenomena) are empty of any inherent or distinctive attributes. He called them emptiness, or *sunyata* in Sanskrit.[2]

Emptiness is a condition of no fixed entity, or of no-selfness. Since each thing exists only by virtue of its opposite, he demonstrates that all things are only relative to other things and are without essence. That is, they are empty.

However, although everything is empty, we still exist and function in the phenomenal world. What, then, is the relationship between the two realms of the absolute and the relative? That is the subject of the Five Ranks and the topic of this book.

o o o o o

When we study the Five Ranks of Tozan in the White Plum lineage, we study them in two different sets. The first is called Hensho Goi, where *hen* means "relative," *sho* means "absolute," and *goi* means "Five Ranks." It is what most people think when they first encounter the Five Ranks of Tozan. Here is my version of the Hensho Goi:

Rank 1: The relative in the midst of the absolute
Rank 2: The absolute in the midst of the relative
Rank 3: Coming in the midst of the absolute
Rank 4: Reaching in the midst of the relative
Rank 5: Arriving in the midst of absolute/relative
    (unity realized)

We'll explore these in detail in this introductory chapter and throughout part two of this book.

There is also a second set of ranks, called Kokun, which roughly means "sequence of merit," and these form the focus of part three. Here is my version of this set of ranks:

Rank 1: Shift
Rank 2: Submission
Rank 3: Achievement or awakening
Rank 4: Collective achievement or collective awakening
Rank 5: Absolute achievement or absolute awakening

The Kokun Goi appear to be a linear representation of Zen practice. First we experience a shift that illuminates the Zen path and encourages us to start to practice. When we shift, we are sticking our toe in the water to test it out. Then there is submission to the teachings and the practice, equivalent to plunging into the water. The third rank represents an awakening experience that often occurs after the shift and the submission. However, this awakening is incomplete. Even though we may have some insight, we have not eliminated our negative habits. We are still bounced around by the karma we have accumulated throughout our lifetime. In the next rank, we begin to experience the oneness of cause and effect and dissolve the barriers that separate us from others. In the rank of absolute awakening, all traces of separation disappear, and our ego-grasping consciousness has dissipated.

But Zen practice is not like a fairy tale where the prince and princess live happily ever after. Our practice is endless, and a serious practitioner needs to be constantly vigilant. Vigilance requires more shifts and more submission and more awakening.

At the age of forty-one, after having had several awakening experiences, the great eighteenth-century Zen master Hakuin had a huge awakening experience while reading the Lotus Sutra. He was reading a section wherein the Buddha cautions his disciple Shariputra against savoring the joys of personal enlightenment and reveals to him the truth of the bodhisattva's mission, which is to continue practice beyond enlightenment—teaching and helping others until all beings have attained salvation.[3] Hakuin realized that there is practice beyond awakening and that there is no end to it. In the Kokun Goi, Tozan reaches the same conclusion.

APPROACHES TO THE RELATIVE AND THE ABSOLUTE

As we will see in later chapters, the absolute and the relative can be considered as quite distinct from one another. The experience of the absolute during meditation can appear quite different from relative worldly activities, such as driving a car. Yet each implies the other by means of mutual interpenetration. The contemporary Zen master Joshu Sasaki, who had a Zen center in the traffic-choked city of Los Angeles, used to ask his students, "How do you realize your true self while driving a car on the freeway?" If you do not see it directly, your response will be nothing but "thoughts that are nowhere supported by anything," as the Diamond Sutra states.

Let's consider these lines from the Heart Sutra (which is the most condensed distillation of the Prajna Paramita Sutra) and relate them to Tozan's Five Ranks:

Form is emptiness.
Emptiness is form.
Form is exactly emptiness.
Emptiness is exactly form.

Here, again, is my version of the first set of Five Ranks:

Rank 1: The relative in the midst of the absolute
Rank 2: The absolute in the midst of the relative
Rank 3: Coming in the midst of the absolute
Rank 4: Reaching in the midst of the relative
Rank 5: Arriving in the midst of absolute/relative
    (unity realized)

Although some of these expressions may seem difficult to grasp at first, as we go through the book, we'll unpack and examine each of them to bring them into greater clarity.

The first rank, "the relative in the midst of the absolute," suggests an experience of reality in which "form is emptiness." According to Nagarjuna, all phenomena, when correctly understood, are nothing other than the manifestation of emptiness. This rank refers to the first awakening experience of the Zen practitioner, often called a *kensho* experience (a term we discuss in more detail at the start of chapter 2), in which one directly perceives phenomena as the manifestation of emptiness.

The second rank, "the absolute in the midst of the relative," represents experience from the polar opposite direction. Emptiness is form. The ultimate reality is present in all places and in all times as all things. Tozan wrote a poem for each Hensho Goi as an expression of that rank, and these verses are ideal metaphors to capture the meaning of these relationships. We'll go through these short poems line by line in the chapters associated with each rank.

The third rank articulates the absolute. It examines the nature of the absolute independent of the relative. In the language of the Heart Sutra, one could say that emptiness is emptiness, or the absolute is the absolute.

The fourth rank articulates the relative. This rank examines the nature of the relative as an entity unto itself. Referring to the previous lines of the Heart Sutra, this rank would be form is form, or the relative is the relative.

We need to thoroughly understand the subtle meaning of each of the preceding ranks in order to experience the fifth rank, which points to the complete harmonious experience of reality that transcends both the absolute and the relative.

In Sino-Japanese, the title of each of the Five Ranks contains the character Chu, which means "middle" or "in the midst of." For instance, it is the same character that appears in the term *chudo*, the Japanese word for the Buddhist "Middle Way." The *kanji* (Japanese rendering of a Chinese character) for Chu clearly shows its "middle" quality pictographically with a line in the middle of a rectangle: 中. In this book, I translate Chu as "in the midst of." Here, for example, is the Sino-Japanese with my translations for the first rank:

Hen—"relative"
Chu—"in the midst of"
Sho—"absolute"

I take other renderings of Chu, such as "containing" or "within," to be mistranslations because one state (relative or absolute) is not larger than the other and therefore cannot contain the other.

Chu is also sometimes translated as "exactly penetrating the point," which can be pictured as an arrow penetrating inside the bull's-eye of a target. Many of our ancient Zen masters talked about turning the light around and shining it back inside oneself. This is also Chu. For example, Rinzai (Ch. Linji Yixuan) wrote, "You must right now turn your light around and shine it on yourselves, not go seeking somewhere else."[4]

Just as we chant in the Heart Sutra that "form is emptiness" and "emptiness is form," we can say that "relative is absolute" and "absolute is relative." One does not contain the other, but for the first two of the Five Ranks, we might say that the absolute harmonizes with the relative and the relative harmonizes with the absolute. In this context, Chu represents harmony or balance. When everything is in balance, then peace and tranquility prevail.

Roshi Bernie Glassman, the founder of the Zen Peacemakers, incorporated his own understanding of Chu into the language of the three Zen Peacemakers Tenets, which are:

1. Not-Knowing, or maintaining the mind of not-knowing
2. Bearing Witness, or bearing witness to the joy and pain in the world
3. Taking Compassionate Action that comes from not-knowing and bearing witness[5]

In shorthand, these are known as not-knowing, bearing witness, and taking action. With regular application, the practice of the three tenets can become a way of living from one's calm center at all times.

Bernie studied Chu as a koan with Sochu Suzuki Roshi and realized that Chu could be the same as bearing witness. He took Chu, "in the midst of," to be another way of saying "presence without judgment." There is healing power in the ability to be present to the pain and joy in the world. When one is bearing witness, there is openness without attachment or judgment.

When I was studying at the Zen Center of Los Angeles in the 1970s, one of the students was an accomplished psychiatrist in West Los Angeles. He told me that the more he practiced meditation, the less he had to say to his patients and the better they got. That is bearing witness and the power of presence.

During conversations Bernie and I had about the Five Ranks, he came up with these translations of the Five Ranks:

The absolute bearing witness to the relative
The relative bearing witness to the absolute
Bearing witness to the absolute
Bearing witness to the relative
Bearing witness to life itself

Life is neither relative nor absolute, and it is neither form nor emptiness. It is just everything as it is, beyond words, beyond letters. Dwelling in no fixed place, supported by nothing.

Let's look at an example from physics to get another angle on how reality eludes our fixed conceptions. In the last century, there was a debate in physics about whether elementary particles are actually particles or waves. Experiments showed that under some circumstances they behaved as if they were particles, and in other circumstances they behaved as if they were waves. Even light, which had been thought to be a series of waves, could be demonstrated to act as if it were particles. And electrons, originally thought to be particles, were shown to have wavelike behavior also.

So, what are they? Particles or waves? Nobel Prize–winning physicist Richard Feynman said that small quantum entities are neither particles nor waves. They are something else. We just don't know what that something else is. Furthermore, since there are no familiar analogies that explain their behavior, we just have to accept that subatomic particles behave in this screwy way.

In a somewhat similar way, we can say that sometimes our perception of reality appears to be absolute. Everything is unified. And sometimes our perception is focused on diversity or the relative. If we then ask what the true nature of reality is, a definitive answer eludes us. Our understanding cannot identify a fixed abiding place. There is no firm ground upon which to stand.

When Zen practitioners are ready to commit to the Buddha Way, they ask to receive the Buddhist precepts and avow their commitment to following the path revealed by the Buddha. The preceptor summarizes the ceremony by saying, "Now that you have received these precepts, the great wisdom is your teacher, and you should not follow dualistic or misleading ways."

The phrase "dualistic ways" implies a state of separation between oneself and other people or between oneself and other things or entities. It would even include creating a separation or gap within oneself, such as giving credence to the inner critic who judges you and your abilities and actions, and internally comments on whether you are loveable or not.

From a Buddhist perspective, creating a separation between God and human beings—or between any characterization of the absolute and relative or phenomenal worlds—is dualistic and misleading. In general terms, the absolute can be identified with God or Buddha Nature, and the relative with human beings and everything in the phenomenal world.

According to some teachings of theistic religions such as Christianity, Judaism, and Islam, God is a separate entity who passes judgment and grants grace. We can thus find innumerable examples of God portrayed as angry, jealous, benevolent, loving, personal, or impersonal. In the context of our discussion in this book, however, God is the absolute. Some Buddhists believe in God or gods, yet in Buddhism, even deities cannot be seen as separate from human beings.

Not all Christians, Jews, or Muslims see God as separate from humans. In the Bible, Jesus says, "The kingdom of God is within you" (Luke 17:21). One does not enter the kingdom; one *is* the kingdom, because in the absolute there are no opposites, no inside and no outside. From this standpoint, the practice of Christianity would be to realize how your life manifests as the kingdom of God.

One of the most well-known adherents of Sufism, the mystical branch of Islam, is the poet Rumi. He said, "In real existence there is only unity."[6] And the Jewish mystic Rabbi Baal Shem Tov wrote, "Once man is aware that everything is God—one of the fundamental secrets is—there is no more separation."[7]

Nonetheless, we know from certain experiences that everything is not one—or in other words, that we cannot simply resolve all problems into the absolute if we want to continue to pursue our lives. Others can insult and injure us. If we don't look both ways before crossing the street, we can be hit by an "other" in the form of a car or bus. This quandary was well known in ancient China, as recorded in collections of dialogues between Zen masters and their disciples. These exchanges are called koans. Koans are used in Zen training to expand and clarify the insight of Zen students, including the types of questions about the relative and absolute that are central to Tozan's Five Ranks.

In case 100 of a collection of koans known as *The Book of Equanimity*, a monk asked Kaku Osho of Roya (Ch. Langya Jiao), "If the original state is clear and pure, then why suddenly do rivers, mountains, and the Great Earth arise?"

I take the monk's question to mean, if everything is one, how come there are all of these separate entities or things? What about me? Am I separate or united?

Let's reflect on the question "Who am I?" This is one of the basic koans that we offer to students who are just starting to study koans. An uninitiated person might say, "I am this body and this mind." But if you had a limb amputated, would the essence of who you are be diminished? Is your mind of today the same mind you had as a child? Since mind and body are always in flux, you might decide that you are not your mind or your body. Then you might move to your relationships and activities: "I am a son. I am a sister. I am a mother. I am a chef. I am a musician. I am an American." Yet all of these relationships and activities are temporary and transient. Surely none of these could constitute an independent, freestanding, lasting self.

Am I my memories? My thoughts? My feelings? If this question grabs you, you also are probably grappling with how you want to engage in this life that you have been blessed with. These are deep and valid questions of the sort that bring many people to Zen practice.

The Indian sage Ramana Maharshi said, "The question, 'who am I?' is not really meant to get an answer, the question 'who am I?' is meant to dissolve the questioner."[8] Wow, that turns the question around.

Ramana Maharshi's teaching reminds me of the famous words of the thirteenth-century Japanese Zen master Dogen in a fascicle from his masterwork, *Shobogenzo*, entitled "Genjokoan" ("The Way of Everyday Life"):

To study Zen is to study the self.
To study the self is to forget the self.
To forget the self is to be enlightened by all
   phenomena.

To forget the self means that our notions about self are not necessary to live a fulfilling and useful life. If we can let go of our attachments to our ideas of self, then everything we do and everything we encounter reveals the enlightened life.

Let's consider a simple question: How big are you? Through the process of meditation, or *zazen* as it is called in Zen Buddhism, you may begin to experience the dissolution of the self-imposed limits of the body. You might begin to feel boundless—as big as all space—and you also might begin to feel infinitesimal—as if you are contained in a grain of sand. Then as you arise from your meditation seat, you bang your head on a shelf. You are immediately thrown into the reality that your boundless body cannot occupy the same space as other objects.

So, which is it? Are you infinite or finite? The answer has to include both. From the absolute perspective, you are without limit. From the relative perspective, you are limited by the size of your body.

The Transmission of Light (*Denkoroku*) is a collection of koans compiled by Zen Master Keizan Jokin in the fourteenth century. The koans are the enlightenment experiences of all the Zen ancestors in the Soto lineage, starting with Shakyamuni Buddha, continuing through the Indian and Chinese ancestors, and ending with the Japanese ancestors Dogen Eihei and his successor Koun Ejo. When the Buddha was enlightened, according to the first case in *The Transmission of Light*, he proclaimed, "I and all beings everywhere are simultaneously enlightened!" When the Buddha proclaimed that everyone was simultaneously enlightened, he realized his connection with all beings everywhere, and he realized that "he" was "they" because there is no separation—he was boundless. That is realization of the absolute.

I am sure you have experienced the absolute. It is quite common while engaging in a physical activity such as sports or playing a musical instrument. You get so engaged with what you are doing that you dissolve into it. When you are skiing or rock climbing, you become the mountain. There is no separation between you and the mountain, and you reach a state where you are not thinking. You are doing, and even the "you" that is doing seems to have disappeared. There is only skiing or only rock climbing. It is doing without a doer.

In Zen, when you experience this dissolution of self deeply enough, we call it a kensho. It is a first awakening. But as one spiritual pundit put it, "After awakening, the laundry." We still have our life in the relative world. We have to take care of the dirty laundry; take care of the children; and earn enough money to provide food, shelter, and clothes. As Dogen says, when we forget the self, this relative life is also the enlightened life.

How do we bring meditation into life? When Bernie Glassman started meditating with Maezumi Roshi, he asked about the meaning of walking meditation, or *kinhin*. Maezumi Roshi said, "When you walk, just walk." Bernie later said that the simplicity and profundity of Maezumi Roshi's answer convinced him that he was in the right place. How easy to expound it, and yet not so easy to do it.

THE LIFE OF ZEN MASTER TOZAN

Who was Tozan, the author of the Five Ranks? With his student Sozan (Ch. Caoshan Benji), he is recognized as the founder of the Soto (Ch. Caodong) school of Zen, one of the two main branches of Zen continuing to this day.

Tozan knocked around for a while until, at the age of thirty, he visited the Zen masters Nansen (Ch. Nanquan Puyuan) and then Isan (Ch. Guishan Lingyou). Tozan had read about the "teaching of the insentient" and asked Isan about it but was not able to understand his meaning. Isan recognized Tozan as a student of ability and sent him to another master, Ungan (Ch. Yunyan Tansheng), where the following dialogue took place:

TOZAN: "Who can hear the preaching of the Dharma by the insentient?"
UNGAN: "The insentient can hear it."
TOZAN: "Your reverence, do you hear it?"

UNGAN: "If I were to hear it, you would not hear my preaching."

TOZAN: "Why do I not hear it?"

Raising the whisk, Ungan said: "Do you hear it?"

TOZAN: "No."

UNGAN: "When you don't hear even my preaching, how can you hear that of the insentient."

TOZAN: "On what work is the phrase 'teaching of the insentient' based?"

UNGAN: "In the Amida sutra it says, 'The streams, the birds, the trees, the groves, all chant the name of the Buddha.'"

At these words Tozan attained some understanding and composed this verse:

How wonderful, how very wonderful
The preaching of the insentient is inconceivable
Listening with the ear, it is difficult to
    understand
Hearing with the eye, then you can know it

When Tozan took leave of Ungan, he asked him what he should say if asked, "Can you still recall your master's true face?"

The master remained silent for a while and then replied, "Just this one is."

After another pause, Ungan said, "In carrying out this charge, exercise your utmost circumspection and care."[9]

Later, Tozan had a further realization of "Just this one is" while looking at his reflection in a stream. He composed another gatha, or short verse:

> Do not seek him anywhere else!
> Or he will run away from you!
> Now that I go on all alone,
> I meet him everywhere.
> He is even now what I am.
> I am even now not what he is.
> Only by understanding this way
> Can there be a true union with the Self.[10]

This gatha is reminiscent of a long verse called *The Song of the Jewel Mirror Samadhi* (see appendix C) that has been attributed to Tozan. In Japanese it is called *Hokyozanmai*, and it is chanted regularly in Zen monasteries and temples. However, in *The Record of Tozan*, a compilation of his sayings and doings, it is written that Tozan learned *The Song of the Jewel Mirror Samadhi* from his teacher, Ungan Dogo, in secret, and that he transmitted it to his successors. The whole verse is reproduced in *The Record of Tozan*.[11]

> *The Song of the Jewel Mirror Samadhi* states:
> The dharma of suchness is intimately transmitted
>   by buddhas and ancestors.
> . . . .
> You are not it, but in truth it is you.

Your notion of who you are is too small to encompass the Dharma of suchness. But the Dharma of suchness encompasses you. One way to look at it is that from the relative perspective, you are different from everyone else. Thus, you are not it. But the Dharma of suchness does not exclude anything because it represents the absolute perspective. It completely subsumes you and everything about you.

In case 50 of *The Book of Equanimity*, Ganto (Ch. Yantou Quanhuo) said about his close Dharma brother, Seppo (Ch. Xuefeng Yicun), "We were born of the same branch, but we will not die of the same branch." By being born, he is referring to their awakening experience. In other words, their experience of the absolute was "of the same branch." Yet, even after awakening, they appear differently in the world, so they "will not die of the same branch." They both experienced the absolute, which was the same experience for both of them, but their expression of that experience reflects their own unique personalities. In truth it is them, but they are not it.

Here is a different translation of the verse Tozan wrote after he was awakened upon seeing his reflection in the water of a stream:

Just don't seek from others, or you'll be far
    estranged from self.
I now go on alone; everywhere I meet it.
It now is me; I now am not it.
One must understand in this way to merge with
    suchness.[12]

Why can Tozan say, "It now is me. I now am not it"? Because there is no "I" to be it. It is the new I. What is "it"? It is the it that he meets everywhere he goes. It is the Dharma of suchness. Try to grab it, and it disappears in a puff of smoke. Just do the laundry.

Many of the entries in *The Record of Tozan* have been compiled into traditional koan collections. I want to use one as an example of how to work with koans, since the Five Ranks are best understood when they are treated as koans.

When I worked at the Scripps Institution of Oceanography, we developed apparatus that would allow a deep-sea diver to remain warm. We tested it in a tank that was about forty feet deep and contained cold water drawn from the deep ocean; the water was kept continually circulating. I was one of the subjects in these tests. With probes all over my body, I went to the bottom of the tank while my core body temperature, blood pressure, and other variables were measured. While I was floating near the bottom of the tank, I thought of case 43 in *The Blue Cliff Record*, "Tozan's Hot and Cold."

A monk in all earnestness asked Master Tozan, "How do you avoid the discomfort of hot and cold?"

Master Tozan said, "Go to that place where there is no hot and cold."

The monk said, "Where is that place?"

The Master replied, "When you are hot, be hot and when you are cold, be cold."

"When you are cold, be cold." Since I was not wearing a wet suit, it was very cold. I asked myself, "What's cold?" I totally experienced the cold. With each breath, my whole universe was a feeling of cold penetrating my whole body.

Most of the subjects had to leave the water after twenty minutes because their body temperature dropped too low. I was sitting there concentrating on the cold, and after an hour they finally told me to come up. My body temperature had barely dropped. The naval officer who was running the tests said, "What were you doing down there?" I replied, "Nothing." But after that experience, I didn't get cold for the longest time. I really understood Tozan's hot and cold. Just really be cold. Really be hot. Who's hot, and who's cold? Forget the self and just be cold. Then the cold disappears.

We could use this approach for dealing with feelings such as sadness, grief, and guilt. When you are sad, be sad. When you are grieving, just grieve. Feel the feeling thoroughly with your whole body. Forget the self and just be sad. Then even the sadness disappears.

To further illustrate koan study, I use the example of the dialogue between the contemporary Zen master Soen Nakagawa and a Christian scholar. While they were having tea, Soen asked, "What were the last words of Christ on the cross?"

The scholar said, "My God, my God, why have you forsaken me?"

Soen said, "No, he did not say that."

The scholar disagreed and said, "Yes, that is what he said."

Again, Soen said that Christ did not say that.

Finally, getting annoyed, the scholar said to Soen, "Then you tell me what he said."

Soen stood up and flung his arms out wide as if he were hanging from the cross and said in a mournful voice, "My God, My God. Why have you forsaken me?"

Do you see the difference? The scholar was reciting detached knowledge, and Soen embodied Christ at that moment. As we study the Five Ranks, bear in mind the difference between a scholarly approach and a Zen approach to manifesting yourself as the Five Ranks.

Here is a final anecdote about Master Tozan that I want to share at this juncture.

One day, Tozan ordered his head to be shaved, his bath to be drawn, and a fresh robe to be brought. Then he said farewell to his assembly and passed away. All the monks wailed bitterly.

Suddenly the master opened his eyes and said, "The hearts of men who go forth into the homeless life should not be dependent on things. This is true practice. What use is there in grieving when troublesome life comes to rest in death?"

He then ordered the cooks to prepare a "fools' feast" to rebuke the assembly. Tozan delayed his departure by seven days and finally said, "Why do all you monks behave so rudely? Why do you make such a disturbance when I am on the point of departure?" Then he bathed again, sat erect, and departed.

2

What Is the Absolute?
What Is the Relative?

To realize the absolute is the major challenge one encounters in all spiritual practices. In Zen, to experience the absolute is called kensho. The word *kensho* consists of two characters—*ken*, which means "see," and *sho*, which means "nature"—so to "see one's nature" is the usual translation. *Satori* is a synonym for kensho. They both mean the sudden flashing into consciousness of a new truth hitherto undreamed of.

The story of Chiyono, a thirteen-century Japanese woman who became a famous Zen abbess, illustrates her realization of the absolute. According to legend, Chiyono worked as a servant in a Zen convent and wanted to learn how to meditate and connect with Buddha.

An elderly nun told her, "People are complete as they are. If you don't fall into delusive thoughts, there is no Buddha and no sentient being; there is only one complete nature. If you want to know your true nature, you need to turn toward the source of your delusive thoughts. This is called zazen."

Chiyono practiced zazen meditation diligently for months. One day, she went out on a night with a full moon to draw some water from the well. The bottom of her old bucket, held together by bamboo strips, suddenly gave way, and the reflection of the moon vanished with the water. When she saw this, she attained great realization.[1]

Chiyono had just repaired her bucket, and when it fell apart, her concepts of reality fell apart. She saw how elusive everything is, and she had a powerful experience of the absolute.

Synonyms for *absolute* in Zen include "the True Self," "Buddha Nature," "big mind," "the subtle source," and the single word *mu*. Sometimes we make up words, such as *thusness* and *suchness*. Yet whatever your mind can conceive is not the absolute, which is ineffable.

A monk asked Zen Master Joshu (Ch. Zhaozhou Congshen), "Everything comes from the one. What does the one come from?" (*Blue Cliff Record*, case 45). There is no abstract description that reaches it.

The monk's question reminds me of a question that you might have asked as a child: "If God created everything, who created God?" It is an innocent question, yet adults are afraid to ask it; it is blasphemy in some traditions. Did you ask that question in your religious school? What were you told?

The Zen version of that question is the koan "What is the source of mu?" To realize the source is like exploring a deep cave with a stream flowing through it. What at first may appear to be the source of the stream soon gives way to another chamber, and we need to keep going deeper to find the source.

In looking for the source of mu, whatever we find, we need to determine the source of that. What is the source of our opinions? What is the source of our beliefs, including our belief that "I am an independent autonomous being"? Then, taking all of that together, what is its source? How far can you go? As soon as you think you have found it, there must be a source for that.

The Chinese Zen verse *Trust in Heart/Mind* (*Xinxin Ming*) says,

> If mind does not discriminate, all things are as they
>   are, as One.
> To go to this mysterious source frees us from all
>   entanglements.[2]

What is this mysterious source? In the end, all we can say is that it is a mystery and cannot be known. The absolute is devoid of any fixed attributes. If you think you know what the absolute is, you are fixing it in place and consequently missing its true reality.

The main reason that words fail to reach the full extent of the absolute is because it is an experience and not a concept. It is possible to hint at the absolute by trying to capture the experience with words, but ultimately it is meaningless unless the listener has had a similar experience.

For example, Master Gensha (Ch. Xuansha Shibei) described the absolute by saying, "The universe is one bright pearl."

A monk asked Gensha, "I've heard you teach that the entire world is one bright pearl. How should we interpret that?"

Gensha replied, "The entire universe is one bright pearl. What is there to interpret or understand?"

Later he said, "You must know that even in the Black Mountain Cave of Demons complete freedom is working." (*Shobogenzo*, "Ikkamyoju" ["One Bright Pearl"])

Gensha had a difficult life, including seeing his father drown in front of him. He was driven by his suffering to become a Zen monk. He studied diligently and eventually experienced the absolute. Because of his tragic life and eventual realization, Gensha was able to say that the entire universe is one bright pearl. He was also able to say that complete freedom is at work even in the Black Mountain Cave of Demons.

When the time is right, you will grasp the essence of the one bright pearl. This pearl is to be found inside your own clothing. Even when situations seem to change, and even when you find yourself in the cave of demons, everything is always the one bright pearl. No actions, speech, or thoughts exist separately from the one bright pearl. It is not bound by thoughts of large or small, adequate or inadequate, negative or positive. One bright pearl is the entire universe. It is your life—but do you know it?

Although it is possible to describe the experience of swimming in the ocean and tasting its salt water to someone who has lived their entire life in the mountains and only ever tasted freshwater streams and lakes, that person can only imagine what the experience is like. No matter how well you describe the ocean's buoyancy and briny taste, they will not truly know what you are talking about until they finally travel to the seashore and immerse themselves in the salty expanse.

This experiential threshold is there even for activities that we do every day without thinking about them. For instance, consider walking. There is no way you can explain the true experience of walking to someone who has never walked and wants to learn. Sure, you could describe the biomechanics, but that's not how we *experience* walking. What do you do when you walk? Do you tell your leg, "Lift up and swing forward?" How do the neurons know to fire and contract and then relax the muscles to create the desired motion? You don't know. You just do it. Yet you did not gain that skill easily.

I'm sure you have seen toddlers first learning to walk. They pull themselves up and try to take a step. Then they lose their balance and fall on the floor or hit themselves on a piece of furniture. After a good cry, they pull themselves up and try again. They do it over and over again until they have the strength and balance to take a few unaided steps. Then they keep at it until they have mastered walking. I have never seen a child give up and decide that it is too difficult. As adults, we cannot explain to someone else how to walk, but we can talk about the intricacies of walking with someone who has also had the experience.

The experience of the absolute is similar to tasting the ocean or knowing what it is to walk. Unless someone else has had the same experience, it is impossible to truly convey it. If you want to experience the absolute, you have to apply yourself, like Chiyono, Gensha, and all of the Zen ancestors.

Describing the absolute, Master Nansen said, "[The Way] is like outer space, so vast and boundless. How can there be right and wrong in the Way?" (*Gateless Gate*, case 19).

Bodhidharma is the First Zen Ancestor. He traveled from India in the fifth century C.E. to take Buddhism to China. The combination of his Indian Mahayana Buddhism and Chinese Taoism gave birth to Zen. When Bodhidharma arrived in China, he was invited to visit Emperor Wu, who asked him, "What is the first holy principle of Buddhism?"

Bodhidharma replied, "Vast emptiness. No holiness." (*Book of Equanimity*, case 2)

In English, when you say, "I feel empty," it means that you are without purpose, hopeless, lost. In Bodhidharma's case, the term carries an entirely different meaning. In Buddhism, *emptiness* means that nothing is fixed. Everything is impermanent, as the Buddha taught. What does *impermanence* mean? It means that nothing is enduring, whether externally or internally. Nothing is secure. As soon as you think you've nailed something down, it has moved. Because everything's impermanent, there's no self.

The absolute is no fixed thing, nothing to grasp on to, no firm ground upon which to stand. Because of that, there's tremendous freedom. Being free, the absolute can manifest in all kinds of ways according to conditions. That is what Bodhidharma expressed to the emperor.

o   o   o   o   o

The Zen tradition has an expression for someone who focuses on the absolute at the expense of the relative: a "board-carrying fellow." Imagine someone walking down the main street of a town carrying a wooden board on one shoulder. The board acts like a visor that shields their view of one side of the street. Then the fellow comments about what a funny town this is—it only has buildings on one side of the street! To complete the picture, we have to consider the relative realm, which includes all phenomena, objects, and their interactions.

The relative realm is usually the realm of our everyday lives in which we have roles to fulfill and decisions to make. When I prepare my breakfast in the morning, I need to make eggs, or oatmeal, or both, or something else. If I try to include *everything* in my breakfast, the breakfast will never take place. The relative is the realm of choices, perspectives, and limitations. I might experience a sense of oneness with a tree, but that does not mean I can metabolize sunshine the way a tree does. I might know that you and I share a profound nature in the absolute, but that doesn't mean you put on my pants in the morning or that I pay your bills for you. The relative realm is a realm of diversity and differences. You are you, and I am me.

The relationship between the absolute state and the relative or phenomenal world is a vexing question. In Zen, it is a critical issue that's taken up in numerous classical writings. The verse *Identity of Relative and Absolute* (*Sandokai*), written by Sekito Kisen (Ch. Xitou Xiqian), includes this couplet:

The subtle source is clear and bright;
The tributary streams flow through the darkness.[3]

The subtle source is a reference to the absolute, while the tributary streams (sometimes translated as "branching streams") refer to the phenomenal, relative world. Thus, these two lines describe *what is* from two perspectives.

The subtle source is clear and bright because it cannot be defiled. In the phenomenal world, we can say that something is defiled, but in the absolute, things are just as they are. The vast sky cannot be defiled by clouds, storms, pollution, or bird shit. Even the buildup of greenhouse gasses in the atmosphere does not defile the open nature of the sky, which simply accommodates them as it has for billions of years; it is from the relative perspective that we say that a certain level of carbon dioxide or methane is "better" than another level. Only in the sphere of dualism, the sphere of the relative, can we talk about something being stained or dangerous.

The tributary streams are constantly flowing. They keep changing shape, color, and clarity. Thus they are a perfect metaphor for the relative. They are also a metaphor for life. Life flows and keeps changing shape, age, and vitality as well as other characteristics. Each of us is like a tributary stream; we are not separate from the ebb and flow of energy in the universe.

The Buddha described that nonseparateness as the inter-dependence of all beings, both animate and inanimate. This realization has been a cornerstone of Buddhist understand-ing and philosophy. The technical term is "codependent origination." Everything arises simultaneously, is informed by everything else, and at the same time informs everything else. We could say that we are all simultaneously picked up by our own bootstraps.

The tributary streams, which represent the relative, flow and merge with the sea, which represents the absolute. Thus every phenomenon has its resting place in the absolute. Then the water evaporates and returns as rain to the streams. So all phenomena, or the relative, arise from the sea of the absolute and return to the sea of the absolute. Furthermore, the tributary streams inform each other, since water mol-ecules that started in one stream circulate through other streams. Eventually it is difficult to distinguish which water molecules belong to which stream.

The mind usually cannot get itself around the notion that everything originates codependently. The basic prob-lem is that one's worldview is distorted. It's based on false assumptions. This point comes across well in the following ancient Indian tale:

Once upon a time, there lived six blind men in a village. One day the villagers told them, "Hey, there is an elephant in the village today."

They had no idea what an elephant was. They decided, "Even though we will not be able to see it, let us go and feel it anyway." All of them went to the elephant, and every one of them touched the great beast.

"Hey, the elephant is a pillar," said the first man, while touching the elephant's leg.

"Oh, no! It is like a rope," said the second man, who touched its tail.

"Oh, no! It is like a thick branch of a tree," said the third man, who touched the elephant's trunk.

"It is like a big hand fan," said the fourth man, who touched its ear.

"It is like a huge wall," said the fifth man, who touched its belly.

"It is like a solid pipe," said the sixth man, who touched one of its tusks.

They began to argue about the elephant, each of them getting agitated as he insisted that he was right. Passing by, a wise man saw what was happening. He stopped and asked them, "What is the matter?"

They said, "We cannot agree as to what the elephant is like." Each one of them then repeated how he perceived the elephant.

The wise man calmly explained to them, "All of you are right. The reason every one of you is telling it differently is that each one of you touched a different part of the elephant. So, actually the elephant has all those features that you described."

"Oh!" they all said. There was no more reason to fight, and they felt happy that they were all right.

Those who have a glimpse of the absolute or emptiness are prone to thinking that it alone constitutes the true
nature of reality. If they were one of the men in the story,
they would say, "The elephant is ineffable oneness." In the
Identity of Relative and Absolute, however, it says, "To encounter
the absolute is not yet enlightenment." It is such a powerful experience to witness the absolute that some people get
stuck there and do not pursue their practice further. Yet
witnessing the absolute is only one aspect of reality, and if
one gets attached to the absolute side, it is a pity. We say that
such a person has caught the stink of Zen.

On the other hand, if we only see the diversity of life with
all its many forms, we might think *that* is the nature of reality.
In this position, we are again like the blind men touching only
one part of the elephant. We still do not see the whole thing.

○　○　○　○　○

An eighth-century Zen teacher named Seigen Ishin (Ch.
Qingyuan Weixin) offered this famous account of his journey through the relative and absolute:

> Before I had studied Zen for thirty years, I saw
> mountains as mountains, and rivers as rivers.
> 　When I arrived at a more intimate knowledge, I
> came to the point where I saw that mountains are
> not mountains, and rivers are not rivers.
> 　But now that I have got its very substance, I am at
> rest. For it's just that I see mountains once again as
> mountains, and rivers once again as rivers.[4]

What is the difference between the first sentence and the last? In both cases, the words say that mountains are mountains and rivers are rivers. Yet Seigen Ishin obviously felt that he had gone through a transition to more intimate knowledge, and having got its very substance, he experienced with clearer eyes. Rather than getting trapped in the absolute view, he returned to the relative world. Everything is the same, yet the way he sees is changed forever.

The Song dynasty Chinese poet Su Shi wrote the following verse found in *Shobogenzo*, "Keiseisansho" ("The Sounds of Valley Streams, the Forms of Mountains"):

> The voices of the river valley are the Buddha's wide
> and long tongue,
> The form of the mountains is nothing other than
> his pure body.

He heard the teaching of the Buddha in the sound of the mountain stream and saw the presence of the Buddha in the shape of the mountains. The absolute and the relative were no longer separate for him. This came after years of meditation practice.

Is water that has been boiled different from unboiled water? Certainly it is if there are pathogens in the original water. Now it is sterilized. Does it taste the same? Chlorine is removed as are some other minerals or chemicals that will affect the taste. But ultimately water is water.

They say that a steel sword that has been beaten and passed through fire multiple times becomes a super steel sword. The fire and beating remove impurities that weaken the crystalline structure of the steel. Yet it is still a steel sword both before and after it is refined.

Seigen Ishin saw mountains before he was awakened, and then he saw mountains after he was awakened. Were they the same or different, or was it his perspective that was different?

As with the story of the blind men and the elephant, it is always possible to view the exact same situation with different eyes and different conclusions. Let's look at a story in a more contemporary setting.

A disquieted man sat in his study. He took his pen and began to write: "Last year I had surgery to remove gallstones. I was bedridden for a long time. In the same year, I turned sixty-five years old and entered retirement age, quitting a job in a company that I loved so much. I had to leave the job I'd been doing for thirty-five years. That same year I was abandoned by my beloved mother, who passed away. Then, still in the same year, my son failed his final medical exam because of a car accident. Repair costs for the car damage were the peak of bad luck last year."

At the end he wrote, "What a bad, bad year!"

The man's wife entered the room and found her husband looking sad and pensive. From behind, the wife saw what he'd written. Slowly, she backed away and out of the room. Fifteen minutes later, she came back in and put down a piece of paper with the following inscription:

"Last year my husband finally managed to get rid of his gallbladder, which had been making his stomach hurt for years. That same year, he was able to retire in a healthy and happy condition. I thank God that he has been given the opportunity to work and earn for thirty-five years to support our family. Now I am grateful that my husband can spend more of his time writing, which has always been his hobby. In the same year, my ninety-five-year-old mother-in-law returned to God in peace and happiness, without any pain. Still in the same year, God protected my son from a terrible accident. Our car was seriously damaged, but my son survived without any ill effects."

In the last sentence, his wife had written, "Last year was a year full of extraordinary blessings from God, and we spent it full of wonder and gratitude."

Reading this profoundly different perspective offered by his wife made the man happy and gave him the energy to start a new writing project. The first sentence said, "In this life we must understand that it is not happiness that makes us grateful. But it is gratitude that will make us happy."

Although the moral of this story comes in a neatly tied bundle, in practice this wisdom is something we have to reveal amidst the messiness of everyday life. The undefiled nature of the absolute presents us with remarkable freedom to reconceive our relationship with the ordinary—and this is one of the topics regularly approached by Zen koans.

A monk once asked Master Ummon (Ch. Yunmen Wenyan), "What is speech that transcends the Buddha and goes beyond the ancestors?"

"Farm rice cake," said Ummon. (*Book of Equanimity*, case 78)

Farm rice cake is a very plain, simple food meant merely to provide some sustenance for workers in the fields of ancient China. Ummon is telling us to work when it is time to work, and when we eat the rice cake, just eat. If we can do that, even the simple fare of a farm laborer would equal that of a five-star restaurant.

A monk asked Ummon, "What is Buddha?"

"A shit stick," said Ummon. (*Gateless Gate*, case 21)

Who would have thought the Buddha is to be found in dirty toilet paper (the modern equivalent of a shit stick)? When you step in gum on the sidewalk or in dog shit on the path, the Buddha is totally present. Who would have thought?

Joshu asked Nansen, "What is the Way?"

Nansen replied, "Ordinary mind is the way." (*Gateless Gate*, case 19)

Our everyday mind is no different from the Enlightened Way. We just have to realize it as such, and then we can find the extraordinary in the ordinary.

What makes ordinary life extraordinary is to live it as something more than a one-way ticket with death as its inevitable destination. The ordinary must lead to the fullness of life and joy that can be expressed as playing in the mystery of life. So, if happiness is the goal and daily activities are the means, then what is the vehicle best suited to reach the goal?

The Chinese Zen adept Layman Pang (740–808) wrote that his daily activities are not unusual and that he is naturally in harmony with them. His supernatural power and marvelous activity is drawing water and carrying firewood.[5]

Washing bowls and filling the washbasin are both Dharma gates, both Buddha's affairs. Dharma gates are omnipresent.

When we vow to enter them, whether pleasant or unpleasant, without reservation, the Buddha's world opens for us.

The modern Vietnamese Zen master Thich Nhat Hanh offered another view of this matter: "Every minute can be a holy, sacred minute. Where do you seek the spiritual? You seek the spiritual in every ordinary thing that you do every day. Sweeping the floor, watering the vegetables, and washing the dishes become holy and sacred if mindfulness is there. With mindfulness and concentration, everything becomes spiritual."[6]

Zen does not confuse spirituality with thinking about God while one is peeling potatoes. Zen spirituality is just to peel the potatoes. That is holy enough.

o   o   o   o   o

We live our lives in a never-ending display of both oneness and diversity. Are they the same or different? Are they one or two, or are they not-one and not-two? If we want to be free, we actually have to let go of the very thing we want to know in order to know it. We have to be willing to forget ourselves utterly and die into that ungraspable mystery. From then on, we have to be willing to live in a state of unknowing, a state in which we don't know who we are. To live in this unknowingness is to dwell intimately in the very heart of that ungraspable mystery. The very part that wants to know will never know the answer.

When there is no distinction between the inherent True Self and its expression in the world of space and time, that is the identity of relative and absolute. This is the most important matter, as it points to the True Self that transcends the narcissism and attachments of the ego, as well as to the innumerable expressions of that True Self as perfection beyond duality.

Edward Conze, a contemporary scholar of Buddhism, wrote of the absolute and emptiness this way:

Emptiness is not a theory, but a ladder which reaches out into the Infinite, and which should be climbed, not discussed. It is not taught to make a theory, but to get rid of theories altogether.[7]

PART TWO

THE FIVE RANKS OF THE ABSOLUTE AND THE RELATIVE

AT THE BEGINNING of each Hensho Goi chapter, I list several translations of the title Tozan gave that rank, as well as poems that are available in the literature for that rank. This way, you will be able to see how different translators render the Chinese text in English.

I should reiterate that these teachings are treated as koans in the White Plum lineage. In each case, the first koan is the title of the rank. For instance, how would you present the title of the first rank, "the relative in the midst of the absolute," without being conceptual?

In the five chapters that follow, we will deal with each of the titles as koans and then each line of the associated verse as a koan.

In my commentaries, I mostly use the translations by Charles Luk, though at times I tweak them or create my own translation based on my understanding of Master Tozan's intent as acquired through my studies with Maezumi Roshi.

3

First Hensho Goi

The Relative in the Midst of the Absolute

THE REAL CONTAINING THE SEEMING
Early in the evening before the moon shines
No wonder they meet without knowing each other.
For still hidden is their mutual aversion.
(Luk, Ch'an and Zen Teaching)

PHENOMENA WITHIN THE REAL
At the beginning of the night's third watch, before
    there is moonlight,
Don't be surprised to meet yet not recognize
What is surely a familiar face from the past.
(Powell, The Record of Tung-shan)

THE PHENOMENON WITHIN THE UNIVERSAL
When the third watch begins, before the moon rises,
Don't think it is strange to meet and not recognize
    the other,
You still somehow recall the elegance of ancient days.
(Aitken, The Morning Star)

In the third watch of the night before the moon
  appears.
No wonder when we meet there is no recognition.
Still cherished in my heart is the beauty of earlier
  days.

(Miura and Sasaki, *Zen Dust*)

As we begin our exploration of the first rank, please remember that although the phrase "Five Ranks" implies a progression, each rank contains the others. This first rank, in particular, supports all the others, and they are included within it.

Tozan's verse for the first rank states:

Early in the evening before the moon shines
No wonder they meet without knowing each other.
But there is still the fascination of earlier beauty.

In this first rank, the student experiences the realm of emptiness. Hakuin's description says that in deep *samadhi* "with no self-awareness, the empty sky vanishes and the iron mountain crumbles. Above heaven there is not a tile to cover her head, below not an inch of ground for her to stand on."[1] In Zen circles, we regard this as a kensho experience.

During a kensho experience, the delusive passions become nonexistent, and so too do samsara and nirvana. There is not a thought or a notion of enlightenment or delusion. There is no thought or notion of age, gender, race, country of origin, or any other marker of human difference. It is a state of total emptiness without sound or odor, like a bottomless, clear pool.

Zen Master Hakuin said, "The Great Perfect Wisdom Mirror is perfectly revealed, strange to say, as a black lacquer bowl."[2] Light does not emerge from a black lacquer bowl.

You cannot see what this Wisdom Mirror is, and if you try to express it, you keep falling into error. Some practitioners regard this state as the be-all and end-all of Zen practice. To call this attitude an error is too weak a term. If Zen practitioners remain here, they loll complacently in self-absorption and declare everything to be void. This is a prime example of what Sekito meant when he wrote, "To encounter the absolute is not yet enlightenment."

Hakuin said, "He whose activity does not leave this rank falls into the poisonous sea."[3] In another water metaphor, Zen students who cling to this rank are called "stagnant water." As long as they hide in a place of quietude and passivity, they cannot deal with the chaos of the normal world. When they come into contact with conditions of turmoil and confusion, love and hate, they will find themselves helpless, and all of the miseries of existence will press in upon them. As one Buddhist pundit said, "If you think you are enlightened, spend a weekend with your family."

To save the Zen practitioner from this serious illness, Tozan developed the second rank, "the absolute in the midst of the relative." We will appreciate that expedient in the next chapter, but first, let us consider the individual lines of Tozan's poem for this first rank.

Early in the evening before the moon shines

"Early in the evening before the moon shines" is a time when the sky is dark, and it is difficult to see. Some translations say, "at the beginning of third watch," which implies this same darkness. This line is a description of the experience of emptiness in which one drops one's self-image. There is no self and no other, no subject and no object. It is like Hakuin's black lacquer bowl or like a black hole in the center of the galaxy from which no light escapes.

When we open our eyes to this sphere of reality, we see that it is empty because it has no fixed content. It is vast because it is without limit. If we set up any kind of boundary, that is not this sphere of reality. That is why Bodhidharma, when asked about the first holy principle of Buddhism, said, "Vast emptiness, no holiness." He was talking about this pure sphere of reality.

While raking leaves from the grave of the national teacher, Zen Master Kyogen (Ch. Xiangyan Zhixian) had an awakening experience when he heard the sound of a pebble hitting a piece of bamboo. He wrote the following poem, which accords with this first rank:

> The sound of something struck!—and I have forgotten all I knew.
> Training was not even temporarily necessary.
> In movement and deportment, I manifest the Ancient Way,
> And do not fall into pessimism.
> Nothing of me remains behind when I pass.
> In speech and manner, free of dignity.
> All those who have reached this state of knowledge by experience,
> Without exception tell of this supreme activity-potential.[4]

Even a little bit of realization of the Buddha's enlightenment, such as is experienced when we pass this first rank, can give us great confidence and the faith to continue in our practice. You may have heard the saying "We don't practice in order to become enlightened, but because of enlightenment we practice." Without the enlightenment, what would our practice be?

In case 20 of *The Book of Equanimity*, Master Jizo (Ch. Dizang) said, "Not knowing is most intimate." This state of not-knowing, the most intimate state, is another way of indicating the experience that comes with the first of Tozan's ranks.

As Master Kyogen exclaimed, "The sound of something struck and I have forgotten everything I knew." Not-knowing is most intimate. As soon as we know something, it becomes separate and has a tendency to close off other possibilities. It becomes a piece of knowledge or understanding that we can manipulate. That doesn't mean it's not useful. As human beings, we need that kind of knowledge for many purposes, but it's just not intimate and can't satisfy our deepest longings.

When I was a graduate student in physics, I often was stumped by a problem I was trying to solve. I would try all kinds of techniques and approaches that would end in failure. When I didn't know where to turn, I would give up and sit quietly, not thinking of anything in particular. It was during these moments that the correct approach would suddenly pop into my mind. In his autobiography, the Nobel laureate Luis Alvarez wrote how his father told him to "just sit and think" whenever he was working on a problem.[5] Alvarez discovered many important principles in physics during his "contemplative meditation." In contrast, near the end of his creative life, the Nobel laureate Wolfgang Pauli complained, "Ach! I know too much!" He was not able to quiet his mind and open it to new paradigms.

Not-knowing is most intimate, yet we've developed all kinds of patterns and habits that prevent us from being intimate with ourselves and with others. It's so hard to see these patterns because they're in our blind spots. We just do things without even being aware that we are doing them. They are so much our habitual way of behaving that we don't even recognize them.

In the 1970s, I worked with Professor John Isaacs at the Scripps Institution of Oceanography in La Jolla, California. Professor Isaacs often used to say that there is no tyranny as great as the tyranny of the first successful solution. This tyranny reared its head when we were asked by the U.S. Navy to help develop methods to keep undersea divers warm when they dove to deep depths. The navy's Hot Wet Suit program was looking for solutions to keep the water around the diver's body warm. Professor Isaacs and I showed that divers lost most of their heat through their lungs, not through their skin. We presented a solution that kept the divers warm by moisturizing and heating the air they breathed. But the navy rejected it since it did not involve a "hot wet suit."

Our habits, patterns, and thoughts can easily become the tyranny of our first successful solution. Part of the problem is, we have some kind of image that we want to project and protect. That image is just another way of habitually behaving. We've learned that if we behave in a certain way, and people think about us in a certain way, then somehow we're safe. That's our comfort zone. We struggle to hold on to these old, outdated formulas for behavior, even though they don't really correspond to the reality of the moment or support a wholesome life. They don't provide much useful direction in our practice. To practice is to step into this unknown. This not-knowing is the most intimate of all things.

We can use the struggles that come up as opportunities for awakening. We can bring forth our finest qualities in dealing with difficulties. This inner shift can only occur when our inner questions motivate us and really touch us personally so that we want to manifest this not-knowing.

By honoring not-knowing instead of fighting it, we can discover new possibilities in the midst of our problems. When we think we know all the answers, we feel safe. But life is not safe. We're all going to die. It's a journey into the unknown.

When Jizo said, "Not knowing is most intimate," his student Hogen (Ch. Fayan Wenyi) was enlightened. When you hear about this koan case and that Hogen was enlightened, you can get stuck thinking not-knowing is the Way. You can get stuck anywhere. Not-knowing can just become another habit, another principle. When Jizo said, "Not knowing is most intimate," it covered heaven and earth and was supported everywhere. When you affirm, affirm totally, but don't settle down in affirmation. When you deny, deny totally, but don't get stuck in denial.

Jizo's "not knowing is most intimate" is a very big not-knowing. So big that it contains both knowing and not-knowing. It contains both and neither, all together. As Nansen said, "The Way is not in knowing or in not knowing. Knowing is false consciousness, not knowing is indifference." (*Gateless Gate*, case 19)

We want to function freely in all the realms available to us as human beings. However, by the time we reach adulthood, we're well conditioned to believe that "knowing" is our primary stance toward life. But life is a great mystery, and this stance often leaves us feeling incomplete. When we truly experience the intimacy of not-knowing for ourselves, we become free to choose whichever stance is most appropriate to a given situation.

The commentary to case 20 in *The Book of Equanimity* notes that another Zen master, Cizhou, said, "In walking and sitting, just hold to the moment before thoughts arise. Look into it, and you'll see not seeing. Then, put it to one side." In other words, if you see not-seeing, or hear not-hearing, put it to one side. Don't attach to that. "When you direct your efforts like this," Cizhou continued, "rest does not interfere with meditation, and meditation does not interfere with rest."[6] Before thinking, what is it? That's most intimate.

Everything has fallen away. Previously I wanted to save the world. But alas, early in the morning before the moon shines, I see that there is no world to save.

No wonder they meet without knowing each other

When we "meet without knowing each other," there is no boundary that separates us from one another or from the world. That is true vulnerability, without which there can be no intimacy.

At first glance, you might think that this line of Tozan's verse is not very profound, especially if he is referring to the meeting of strangers who obviously do not know each other. But it extends far beyond that to suggest that you can meet without knowing people you have met before, meet without knowing yourself, and meet without knowing all manner of phenomena. When "they meet without knowing each other," it can give rise to an intimacy that leads to deep insights.

Zen Master Reiun (Ch. Lingyun Zhiqin) was enlightened by seeing falling peach blossoms. Kyogen, whose verse I mentioned earlier, was enlightened by hearing the sound of a pebble striking bamboo. Dogen relates the stories of Reiun and of Kyogen in the *Shobogenzo* fascicle "Keisei Sanshoku" ("The Sound of the Valley Stream, the Color of the Mountain").

Kyogen studied under Isan, who saw in him great possibilities and wanted to open his Zen eye. So, one day, Isan called Kyogen into his room and told him, "I don't want to know about everything you learned from books. Just tell me now who you were before you were born." Completely puzzled, Kyogen couldn't answer. Everything he knew he had learned from books, and that question was not in his books. He desperately kept searching the books for an answer, and he came back to Isan with brilliant answers, but Isan rejected them over and over. Completely exhausted, he came to Isan once more and begged him, "Please teach it to me." But Isan told him, "Even if I teach it to you, it would be my word, and it would have nothing to do with yours."

Kyogen, now even more desperate, took all his books and burned them, saying, "Pictures of cake do not satisfy one's hunger." He took leave of Isan and started on a pilgrimage. Kyogen visited the grave of the national teacher Echu (Ch. Nanyang Huizhong) and decided to stay there as the grave keeper. His inner struggle intensified, continuing day and night. His mind was so still that the lightest touch could become a great explosion. These were the conditions on the day when he was raking the yard and heard a little pebble touch the bamboo. That slight noise opened his mind, and he was deeply enlightened. We could say that Kyogen met the bamboo, the pebble, and himself without "knowing" them. Forgetting all he knew was a great experience of intimacy, with no separation between subject and object. He burst out in laughter, went to his hut, changed his clothes, burned incense, and prostrated in the direction of Isan, saying, "The compassion of Isan is greater than that of my parents. If he had taught it to me, I could never have this great joy today."

Manifesting "the Ancient Way," as he wrote in his enlightenment verse, he went back to sweeping and cleaning. He had to function in the world, or his insight would be of little or no use.

Zen Master Reiun practiced the Way for over thirty years. Once, on a spring pilgrimage, he rested by a village in a spot surrounded by peach blossoms. Upon seeing the blossoms fall, he suddenly attained the Way. We could also say that he met the blossoms without knowing them.

To commemorate his experience, Reiun composed this poem:

> For thirty years I have looked for a sword master.
> Many times leaves fell, new ones sprouted.
> One glimpse of peach blossoms—
> now no more doubts, just this.

Koun Ejo, Dogen's successor, recorded his teacher's words about Kyogen and Reiun:

> The flowers bloom every year, nevertheless, not everyone attains enlightenment by viewing them. Stones often strike bamboo, still not everyone who hears the sound clarifies the Way. Only through the virtue of long study and continuous practice with the assistance of diligent effort in the Way does one realize the Way or clarify the mind. This did not occur because the sound of bamboo was especially wonderful, nor because the color of peach blossoms was particularly profound. Although the sound of bamboo is marvelous, it does not sound of itself; it cries out with the help of a pebble. Although the color of peach blossoms is beautiful of themselves; they open with the help of the spring breeze.
>
> The condition of practicing the Way is also like this. This Way is inherent in each of us; still, our

gaining the Way depends upon the help of fellow practitioners. Though each person is brilliant, still, our practicing the Way needs the power of other people in the sangha. Therefore, unifying your mind and concentrating your aspiration, practice and seek the Way together.[7]

o   o   o   o   o

The first of the three tenets of the Zen Peacemaker Order, founded by Bernie Glassman, is "not-knowing" or "Maintain the mind of not-knowing." When we meet someone, either familiar or unfamiliar, we have all kinds of preconceptions about them. For those with whom we are familiar, we know that they are typically anxious or angry or in good humor, and we bring those memories into the encounter. For those with whom we are unfamiliar, we see that they are missing some teeth, or they wear expensive, stylish clothes, or they are overweight, and we make assumptions based on those observations. How can we encounter our world with a mind of not-knowing so that each moment is fresh and replete with boundless possibilities?

A monk asked Zen Master Razan (Ch. Luoshan Daoxian), "When in front of you is a ten-thousand-foot cliff, and behind you are tigers, wolves, and lions, then what?"

Razan said, "Be there!"[8]

Once at a public talk, a person in the audience asked Roshi Bernie Glassman, "What does it take to live in the here and now?" Without any hesitation, Bernie said, "Everyone who is not living in the here and now, please stand up."

Razan's "Be there" is telling us that we are in the here and now—and this is where we can find our still point and hold to the center.

One of the best descriptions of not-knowing as it's practiced in the Zen Peacemaker Order comes from Roshi Egyoku Nakao:

> The first of the Three Tenets, Not-Knowing, can be described as the letting go of fixed ideas about yourself, others, and the universe. Difficult circumstances—political upheaval, the sudden loss of a loved one, or the unexpected termination of your job—can make life feel suddenly unstable. But actually, according to the Buddha, things are always unstable. It's just that we have a tendency to live life from a set of unquestioned beliefs that make our lives feel solid: we believe that politics will always operate along the status quo, for instance, or that our children will outlive us, or that our plans for the future will come to fruition. The truth is, once you start to pay careful attention to the nature of life, you will begin to question all of your beliefs. How can you know what will happen next? You can't—because the universe, from its tiniest particles to its largest forms, is continually in flux.
>
> In Three Tenets practice, not-knowing trains you to continually set aside fixed points of view. Not-knowing is a flash of openness or a sudden shift to being present in the moment. This dropping away

of the things you have relied upon for a sense of stability may lead you to examine what you believe is your center.

It should be said that the not-favoring-of-viewpoints that arises when one practices not-knowing does not demonstrate a lack of caring. Rather, not favoring any one thing over another allows you to center yourself within a boundless net of interconnection and to expand your circle of caring. In this way, the practice of not-knowing can align you with the ever-changing interconnected reality called Life.[9]

"They meet without knowing each other." Not-knowing is not a place to hide but rather one brimming with possibilities to keep moving in a most wholesome way.

But there is still the fascination of earlier beauty.

You don't have to be a megalomaniac to be narcissistically smitten with yourself. Everyone has an attachment to some version of themselves. Tozan says that even though one has had an awakening experience, there is still an attachment to self in the form of a fascination with our image of who we think we were. Maezumi Roshi renders Tozan's line as "the fascination of earlier beauty." Holding on to that fascination will dispel your insight faster than a speeding bullet.

Carl Jung said that there is no coming to consciousness without pain.[10] People will do anything, no matter how absurd, to avoid the pain of facing their own souls. Unfortunately, one has to enter the dark cave of demons in order to illuminate it.

In Zen, we say that the root of all our delusion is our "self-grasping ignorance." Even though we may have seen through such ignorance in the evening before the moon shines, it is still hanging around. After all, we are discussing the first stage. There is still more to clarify.

Suppose you have a great ship, which can hold ten thousand bales of rice, moored and ready for sailing. A favorable wind is blowing. The rowers are ready, their voices raised in song, really eager to go. The captain, officers, and crew are all in accord, and they set out over the waves for far-off lands, ready to proceed bravely onward day after day. Each day, though they exhaust all their effort, they cannot cross over the rolling waves and instead remain in harbor. Someone forgot to untie the line that moors the ship to the wharf. It is but a small line that holds them, yet it is stronger than ten thousand men.

Day after day, we meditate on the cushion. We work hard, we concentrate, yet somehow we may find that we are still in the harbor. What is that small line that keeps us anchored to the wharf? It's the root of our delusive thoughts. It's that instant of ignorance that has come down through endless eons of time. Everything is made to appear because of its power. Although it's nothing but delusion, it can stifle our zazen more effectively than an army of ten thousand demons. If you examine it carefully, it always comes down to this one belief—that the self is real, that "I" exists separate from everything else. This is our self-grasping ignorance.

No matter how hard we try, as long as we hold on to this belief, we will go nowhere.

Sometimes when we are sitting in meditation, we would rather think about something that's terrible than follow the breath, because at least that terrible thing is ours. The unease we know is safer than the freedom we don't know. And we always love a dramatic story, especially if we are the main character. When we begin to take heed of the discursive mind, that's the first step on the path. And now that the journey has begun, we notice that all of this mental activity is generally designed to protect our ego identification—to protect it from any kind of intrusion so it's safe. Some people find safety in their misery, others in their aggrandizement. It doesn't matter to the ego what it is; what matters is that it feels comfortable and safe, and above all that it helps maintain the delusion of an independent self.

The ego itself can never have an experience of oneness because its very existence depends upon it being separate. Experiences of oneness disturb the ego because they begin to undermine its belief in its own individual, separate existence. Having an awakening experience does not amount to much if the ego grabs it and claims it as its own—and perhaps this is why so many such experiences don't lead to lasting transformation.

"[Awakening experiences] do not in themselves produce wisdom," teaches Jack Kornfield. "Some people have had many of these experiences, yet learned very little. Even great openings of the heart, kundalini processes, and visions can turn into spiritual pride and become old memories. As with a near-death experience or a car accident, some people will change a great deal and others will return to old constricted habits shortly thereafter."[11]

The bottom line is that, in awakening experiences, the "I" is not there. That's the very nature of experiences of nonseparation or oneness. So, "I" have not realized anything. At the end of his life, the Buddha said, "In my 40 years of teaching, I have not uttered a single word."[12] Perhaps you understand what he meant.

For those of us who have had an experience of the first rank but become "stagnant water," reclaiming the spiritual territory that the ego has appropriated requires sharpening our ability to recognize when ego is running the show— when "the fascination of earlier beauty" has taken hold— and being willing to question the assumptions we make on the basis of ego's interpretations and agenda.

There is a legend about Tozan, our protagonist. The gods wanted to see him, but they couldn't because he was so empty of ego attachment that he was invisible to them. They would enter into him or even pass through him, but they could not see him. They were very curious to see a man who had become so empty, so they played a trick on him.

When Tozan had gone for a walk, they went to the kitchen of the monastery where he lived. Taking a few handfuls of rice and wheat, the gods threw them on his path. In the culture of a Zen monastery, which prizes careful alertness, throwing food on the ground is a very disrespectful action. Everything should be respected because everything is alive. When Tozan returned, he could not believe that any of his disciples could have been so careless and disrespectful. This idea arose in him and because he felt offended, suddenly a self was there, and for a moment the gods could see him. He wasn't empty anymore. His reaction had spontaneously crystallized. For a moment, a cloud appeared in the vast blue sky of Tozan's being, and the gods could see him. Then the cloud disappeared because his reaction disappeared. The gods again couldn't see him. Tozan had no hooks that could be grabbed and yanked—at least, not for very long. He knew how to find equanimity in the midst of his own reactivity.[13]

o o o o o

As I've said, each line of Tozan's verse is a koan. How would you present your understanding of them without using conceptual thoughts?

THE RELATIVE IN THE MIDST OF THE ABSOLUTE
Early in the evening before the moon shines
No wonder they meet without knowing each other.
There is still the fascination of earlier beauty.

o o o o o

PRACTICE QUESTION
What beauty from your earlier life still fascinates you and holds you captive?

4

Second Hensho Goi

The Absolute in the Midst of the Relative

THE SEEMING CONTAINING THE REAL

At dawn an old ignorant woman finds her ancient
mirror

Wherein she sees clearly her face which cannot be
elsewhere

No more will she reject her head by grasping at its
shadow.

(Luk, *Ch'an and Zen Teaching*)

THE REAL WITHIN PHENOMENA

An old crone, having just awakened, comes upon an
ancient mirror.

That which is clearly reflected in front of her face is
none other than her own likeness.

Don't lose sight of your face again and go chasing
your shadow.

(Powell, *The Record of Tung-shan*)

THE UNIVERSAL WITHIN THE PHENOMENON

An old woman, oversleeping at daybreak, meets the
    ancient mirror,
And clearly sees a face that is no other than her own.
Don't wander in your head and validate shadows
    anymore.

(Aitken, *The Morning Star*)

THE REAL WITHIN THE APPARENT

A sleepy grandma encounters herself in an old
    mirror.
Clearly she sees a face but it doesn't resemble hers
    at all.
Too bad, with a huddled head, she tries to recognize
    her reflection.

(Miura and Sasaki, *Zen Dust*)

ENYADATTA WAS a beautiful maiden who enjoyed nothing more than gazing at herself in the mirror each morning.[1] One day when she looked into her mirror, she found no head reflected there. The shock was so great that she became frantic, rushing around demanding to know who had taken her head.

"Who has my head? Where is my head? I shall die if I don't find it!" she cried.

Though everyone told her, "Don't be silly, your head is on your shoulders where it has always been," she refused to believe it.

"No, it isn't! No, it isn't! Somebody must have taken it!" she shouted, continuing her frenzied search.

At length, her friends, believing her mad, dragged her home and tied her to a pillar to prevent her from harming herself. With her body immobilized, Enyadatta started to feel calmer, her mind achieving a measure of tranquility. Her close friends tried to persuade her that she had always had her head, and gradually she came to half-believe it. Her subconscious mind began to accept the fact that perhaps she was deluded in thinking she had lost her head, though she remained unsure.

Suddenly one of her friends gave her a terrific clout on the head. In pain and shock, she yelled, "Ouch!"

"That's your head! There it is!" her friend exclaimed, and immediately Enyadatta saw that she had deluded herself into thinking she had lost her head when, in fact, she'd always had it.

Feeling elated, she rushed around exclaiming, "Oh, I've got it! I have my head after all! I'm so happy!"

Enyadatta thus experienced something like the rapture of kensho, and her story conveys what a half-mad state that is. To be overjoyed at finding a head you had from the very first is strange, to say the least. Yet it is no less odd to rejoice at the discovery of your Buddha Nature, which you have never been without. The ecstasy is genuine enough, but your state of mind cannot be called natural until you have fully disabused yourself of the notion "I have become enlightened." Mark this point well, for it is often misunderstood.

If the experience of the first rank is akin to Enyadatta's ecstatic response to getting whacked on the head, that of the second rank is about moving into the awareness that one's head was never gone in the first place.

When your delirium of delight at discovering your essential nature recedes, taking with it all thoughts of realization, you settle into a truly natural life, and there is nothing strange about it. Until you reach this point, however, it is impossible to live in harmony with your environment or to continue on a course of true spiritual practice.

o   o   o   o   o

I translate the second rank as "the absolute in the midst of the relative." Again, the relative is not larger than the absolute, and the absolute is not larger than the relative. One cannot contain the other, and one is not within the other. They comingle.

It is said that the universal nature wisdom is revealed in this rank—revealed precisely through one's discernment of differences. Through this wisdom, a bodhisattva sees beyond all superficial differentiations and perceives the fundamental nature of all things as sunyata, or emptiness. They realize the equality of all beings. Hence, the second rank is also understood as the wisdom of equality or impartiality.

In the first rank there remains a feeling that Buddha Nature is separate from oneself. One's view is still cloudy. In this second rank, we realize that we invariably lead our lives in the realm of all kinds of ever-changing differentiation, what in Buddhist terms is referred to as the realm of the six dusts. Thus, old and young, honorable and vile, plants and trees, buildings and roads are none other than one's own original true and pure self. Wherever you look, you see a Jewel Mirror reflecting your own face.

In *Shobogenzo*, "Genjokoan," Dogen said, "To carry the self forward and realize the ten thousand dharmas is delusion; that the ten thousand dharmas advance and realize the self is enlightenment." When you carry the self forward to realize the ten thousand dharmas, what self is it? When the ten thousand dharmas are seen clearly, there is no self that is seeing them. That is why Dogen says that when the self is carried forward, it is delusion. When the ten thousand dharmas advance and affirm the self, that self can be affirmed because it is no self. When the Buddha touched the earth and said that the Great Earth was witness to his awakening, the ten thousand dharmas affirmed his true self because the self is none other than the ten thousand dharmas.

When Dogen studied with his teacher Tendo Nyojo (Ch. Tiantong Rujing), Nyojo instructed his monks to drop off body and mind. Dogen took that teaching to heart and experienced mind and body dropping off. He went to Nyojo and proclaimed, "Body and mind have dropped off."

Nyojo said, "If body and mind have dropped off, who is this standing before me?"

Dogen said, "The dropped-off body and mind." (*Transmission of Light*, Fifty-first Ancestor)

The first rank of the Hensho Goi is the dropping off of body and mind. The second rank is the dropped-off body and mind.

Hakuin explained that at this second stage, one leaves the realm of emptiness and enters the realm of all kinds of differentiation, and all the differentiations are regarded as one's own original, true aspect. This is called "a white horse enters the reed flowers," or "snow piled in a silver bowl."[2]

The latter expression comes from the chant of *The Song of the Jewel Mirror Samadhi*. The lines read:

A silver bowl filled with snow, a heron hidden in
    the moon.
Apart they seem similar, together they are different.

It is hard to tell which is snow and which is the silver bowl, but the second stage of the Hensho Goi tells you that you must not lump everything together as if it was all the same. You need to discern and appreciate the nature of differences.

This discernment extends to biblical teachings, as well. 1 John 4:1 states, "Beloved, do not believe every spirit, but test the spirits to see whether they are from God, for many false prophets have gone out into the world."

How do we test the validity of what we see, hear, and think? As mentioned in chapter 1, in the Zen *jukai* ceremony of receiving the precepts, the preceptor instructs, "From now on, the Tathagata Buddha, the Complete Enlightenment, and the Perfect Wisdom is your great master. Do not follow misleading or false ways, or people having dualistic understanding."

If there is any separation or dualistic misunderstanding between you and the ten thousand dharmas, it is always the result of a false view and always leads to suffering. These false views give rise to all kinds of prejudice, including racism, homophobia, and misogyny, and they eventually can lead to war. The ten thousand dharmas include everyone and everything, yet it is commonplace to demonize people and groups we perceive as different.

When I lived in London over fifty years ago, there was a short street in the neighborhood that had a few shops, including a greengrocer, a chemist (drugstore), a small grocery store, a small Asian grocery store, and a hardware store. Once when I was shopping in the chemist, the salesclerk was spraying air freshener around the store. I asked her what was going on, and she replied, "A Pakistani was just in here." This experience led me to realize that even foreign smells can give rise to prejudice. Different cultures have diverse tastes in food. Rather than being curious and accepting, many of us judge other people as inferior or even evil if they eat certain things we find strange or distasteful. In Iceland, they eat puffins, one of my favorite birds from my bird-watching days. Can you imagine? In Italy, I have seen sparrows on a skewer in a restaurant window. In northern Vietnam, dogs are considered a delicacy. The thought of it might make a dog-loving Westerner sick—and that same person might wolf down a pork chop for dinner without a second thought.

In this rank, a bodhisattva sees beyond all superficial differentiations and perceives the fundamental nature of all things as emptiness. Thus, they see the equality of all beings independent of race, gender, country of origin, age, disability, religion, and sexual preference.

This profound insight into our shared fundamental nature is not, however, an invitation to spiritually bypass our own hidden prejudices or to ignore societal prejudices due to human differences that give rise to so much suffering in our world. "If we were to simply walk past the fires of racism, sexism, and so on because illusions of separation exist within them, we may well be walking past one of the widest gateways to enlightenment," writes Zen teacher Zenju Earthlyn Manuel. "It is a misinterpretation to suppose that attending to the fires of our existence cannot lead us to experience the waters of peace."[3]

Tozan's verse for the second rank states:

At dawn an old ignorant woman finds her ancient
   mirror

Wherein she sees clearly her face which cannot be
elsewhere
No more will she reject her head by grasping at its
shadow.

Let's look at the lines.

At dawn an old ignorant woman finds her ancient mirror

Dawn is when the light starts to appear after the night of
awakening. We realize that something profound has happened to us, and we begin to bring it to our conscious
mind. As Jung wrote, "One does not become enlightened
by imagining figures of light, but by making the darkness
conscious."[4]

The dictionary definition of *ignorant* is "unaware or unin-
formed." Why is the old woman described as ignorant? It's
not intended as an insult—rather the opposite. Once, when
asked about the purpose of Zen, Maezumi Roshi said, "To
be stupid." Often in our koan study together, he would tell
me that I was being too clever, too sophisticated. Present the
koan so that an uneducated person can understand.

Yakusan Igen (Ch. Yaoshan Weiyan), an eighth- to ninth-
century Chinese master in our lineage, was once challenged
by one of his students. He responded, "I am limping and
palsied, ungainly in a hundred ways, clumsy in a thousand.
Yet I go on this way."[5] Isn't that what we all are? We all have
our capacities, and we are limited in certain ways. My body
no longer allows me to jog, yet I go along this way.

Master Wanshi Shokagu (Ch. Hongzhi Zhengjue) wrote

this verse, referring to Yakusan Igen, in case 69 of *The Book of Equanimity*:

> Limping, limping. Palsied, palsied.
> Frayed, frayed. Unkempt, unkempt.
> . . . .
> Throughout the dharma realm, all becomes his food.
> With drooping nose, he's content to be full.

A drooping nose means that he is a fool, and yet he is full of life and content. Even limping, he is content. Even being an idiot, he is content. Thus, the old ignorant woman finds her ancient mirror wherein she sees her true face. Tozan is encouraging us to reveal our true self. When we see it clearly, we can be as innocent as we are without having to be otherwise. When the mirror is not clear, however, then we still behave at the behest of our ego-grasping ignorance.

In this line of Tozan's verse, then, *ignorant* is a synonym for "not-knowing," in the positive sense, as in having "beginner's mind." It is the ignorance Master Kyogen felt when the pebble struck the bamboo: "The sound of something struck! —and I have forgotten all I knew." This ignorance allows the functioning of wisdom, which is to enter every situation in life with a mind and a heart that are totally open and without prejudgment. It means unconditioned. How can we bring unconditional love to every event and circumstance in our lives?

The ancient mirror was always there but had not been seen. It perfectly reflects everything as it is, adding nothing and omitting nothing. We all have our prejudices that filter reality to make it palatable. If we look at the ancient mirror, none of our projections, attachments, clinging, and judgments reflect in it. It's simply life itself, without anything added.

The narcissistic queen from Snow White would ask her magic mirror daily,

Mirror, mirror on the wall
Who is the fairest of them all?

The ancient mirror, which reflects reality without distortions, tells us that the fairest one of all is everything just as it is. It would answer the queen or anyone for that matter with these lines that I concocted:

How can a mirror find the fairest of all?
It doesn't care if you are short or tall,
Whether you're sloppy or in fancy dress—
'Cuz the ancient mirror is always selfless.

The Song of the Jewel Mirror Samadhi says,

The teaching of Suchness has been intimately com-
    municated by buddhas and ancestors.
Now you have it, so keep it well.
It's like facing a Jewel Mirror.
Form and image behold each other.

Which is form, and which is image? Which is me, and which is you? Now you have it and you have always had it, because it can be no other than you.

Wherein she sees clearly her face which cannot be elsewhere

The man who would become the Sixth Chinese Ancestor, Huineng, was an illiterate layman who found his way to the monastery of the Fifth Ancestor, Hongren. When the Fifth Ancestor was ready to name a successor, he selected Huineng, gave him the ancestral robe and bowl, and then told him that he had better leave since his life was in danger. Sure enough, when the monks heard the news, they were enraged that a layman—and a newcomer at that—could succeed the Dharma from the Fifth Ancestor. The monks started to chase after Huineng, and a former general named Myo finally caught up to him. What happened next is the content of case 23 of *The Gateless Gate.*

The new ancestor, seeing Myo coming, laid the robe and bowl on a rock and said, "This robe represents the faith. How can it be competed for by force? I will allow you to take it away."

Myo tried to lift it up, but it was as immovable as a mountain. Terrified and trembling with awe, he said, "I came for the Dharma, not the robe. I beg you, lay brother, please reveal it to me."

The ancestor said, "Prior to thinking good or evil, what is the original face of Monk Myo?"

In that instant, Myo suddenly attained deep realization, and his whole body was covered with sweat. In tears, he bowed and said, "Besides the secret words and secret meaning you have just revealed to me, is there anything else deeper yet?"

The ancestor said, "What I have preached to you is no secret at all. If you reflect on your own true face, the secret will be found within yourself."

Monk Myo saw his face clearly, which could not be elsewhere.

Here in the second line of the verse, all activity and phenomena are none other than Buddha Nature. "Her face which cannot be elsewhere" is describing the nature of the relative. It is none other than her original face prior to her parents being born.

The Chinese Zen Master Chokei (Ch. Changqing Huileng) wrote the following about his years of meditation practice:

> All I did was to look after an ox. If he got off the road, I dragged him back; if he trampled the flowering grain in others' fields, I trained him by flogging him with a whip. For a long time how pitiful he was, at the mercy of men's words! Now he has changed into the white ox on the bare ground and always stays in front of my face. All day long he clearly reveals himself. Even though I chase him, he doesn't go away.[6]

The ox represents our true self, our Buddha Nature. Our cherished opinions and attachments obscure it from our sight. Chokei is describing his pursuit of the ox, which is also depicted in the famous ten ox-herding pictures. All day long he clearly reveals himself. It is like when Enyadatta recovered her own head.

When you enter this state, "though you push the great white ox, it will not go away."[7] You can try to chase away your true nature, but it will invariably come back.

In his "Song of Zazen," Hakuin said, "All beings are from the very beginning Buddhas. It is like water and ice, apart from water, no ice, outside living being, no Buddhas."[8] Where do we find the Buddha? Hakuin said that they are inside your own clothes. Tozan said that they cannot be elsewhere. If you really believe these masters, your strong faith will bring your Buddha forth.

No more will she reject her head by grasping at its shadow.

An image for this line is two mirrors mutually reflecting each other with no shadow in between. The mind and objects are one, and at the same time, they are not one, not two. There is no subject and no object. Subject and object distinctions have fallen away.

Verses in *Trust in Heart/Mind* state,

> Delusion spawns dualities; these dreams are merely
> flowers of air; why work so hard at grasping
> them?

Can we ever get rid of our bad habits? Or are we doomed to carry them like an albatross around our necks for life after life, death after death?

I have been on the Buddha Path and practicing zazen for almost sixty years. If I did not believe that people can change, and if I had not seen myself and others change through engaging in this practice, I would have found something else to do long ago. For example, through my Zen practice I was able to completely transform my relationship with my mother. She was a very controlling person and smothered her children to keep their lives within the bounds of her wishes and her comfort zone. My reaction in my youth was to tune her out. When I became old enough, I escaped her grasp. I avoided contact with her and tried to live the life I thought I wanted.

The longer I practiced zazen, the more compassionate I felt toward her. I realized that she was gripped by fear and was especially worried that something horrible would happen to her or her children. I began to engage her rather than tune her out. Due to the power of my pure presence, she began to relax. I even found that she had interesting things to say. With my former attitude toward her, I never would have seen that side of her. We had developed a close relationship by the time she died.

One stanza of *Trust in Heart/Mind*, which has been of utmost importance for me in my life, tells us how to transform our bad habits:

Don't go seeking for the truth
Just let those fond opinions go.

When I was younger, I used to be very sarcastic. I did not know it at the time, but I was breaking the seventh Grave

Bodhisattva Precept of "not elevating yourself and putting down others." How did I change? To study Zen is to study the self. I asked myself, "Why do I need to feel superior? To make up for feeling inadequate?" After years of practice and looking deeply at myself, I found that nothing is lacking. The original state is clear and bright! Mountains and rivers suddenly appear! The ancient mirror reflects everything as it is.

When Enyadatta settled down, she was no longer grasping at anything. She went about her business with the confidence of one who has gone through a struggle and emerged clearer and stronger.

So, what's the problem? The problem is that when painful or uncomfortable situations or feelings arise, we think they're not pure. The truth is that they're neither pure nor impure. They just are. But we interpret them in a way that fits into our worldview. If it doesn't fit into that view, then we see it as impure. The basic problem, then, is that one's worldview is impure. It's based on false assumptions. The fundamental assumption is that each of us is an independent, autonomous, unique self, and we need to protect and aggrandize that image at all costs. When we realize the second rank, "the absolute in the midst of the relative," false views dissipate by themselves. We are no longer chasing the ox, and it won't go away.

Yet if one remains here, one does not understand the causal conditions for Buddhahood. One is only a "lesser bodhisattva." What is missing? Hakuin says that understanding of causation, and wisdom that comprehends the unobstructed interpenetration of the manifold dharmas, still needs to be realized.[9]

We'll get to that in the next chapter.

o   o   o   o   o

PRACTICE QUESTION

How has your meditation practice changed you? If you don't know, ask someone close to you. I had a student who proclaimed that he had been meditating for ten years and hadn't changed at all. Some of his longtime friends piped up and said, "You used to be a big mess. Now you are only a small mess."

What kind of mess are *you* now, after taking on meditation practice?

5

Third Hensho Goi

Coming in the Midst of the Absolute

RESURGENCE OF THE REAL
Hard though it be, there is a way to keep free
from dust.
Today's ability to avoid what is forbidden
Surpasses yesterday's most eloquent discussion.

(Luk, *Ch'an and Zen Teaching*)

COMING FROM WITHIN THE REAL
Amidst nothingness there is a road far from
the dust.
If you are simply able to avoid the reigning mon-
arch's personal name,
Then you will surpass the eloquence of previous
dynasties.

(Powell, *The Record of Tung-shan*)

EMERGING WITHIN THE UNIVERSAL

With nothingness, the road is free of dust.
If you can simply avoid mentioning the emperor's
name,
You will surpass the eloquence of the Sui dynasty
poet.

(Aitken, *The Morning Star*)

COMING FROM WITHIN THE REAL

Within nothingness there is a path leading away
from the dust of the world.
Even if you observe the taboo on the present emper-
or's name,
You will surpass that eloquent one of yore who
silenced every tongue.

(Miura and Sasaki, *Zen Dust*)

MAEZUMI ROSHI OFTEN SAID that having a clear realization by itself is of little use. One may have had a dramatic kensho experience (the first rank) and even recovered one's equanimity enough to see clearly that Buddha Nature has been here all along (the second rank) yet still not have put that clear vision into one's everyday life. When this clear insight or wisdom begins to function in one's life, it appears as compassion—and this is one of the hallmarks of the third rank, "coming in the midst of the absolute."

At this stage, the practitioner grows so intimate with the absolute that it becomes second nature. Practitioners of the Buddha Way realize the experience of dwelling in no place and yet functioning in the world. One dwells nowhere, has nothing, and sees the empty nature of all things. Accordingly, one can function freely in the world.

In this state, one is able to see that events and phenomena arise due to conditions and causes. Often the causes are not clear, but the practitioner does not ignore any karmic consequences. They see that everything interpenetrates and affects everything else. They are turned by everything while simultaneously turning everything. What is the nature of this compassionate activity one begins to discover in the third rank?

o   o   o   o   o

The Diamond Sutra states, "Dwelling in no place, raise the Bodhi mind."[1] The bodhi mind is the mind that seeks enlightenment for both oneself and others. It is our bodhisattva vow to receive all sentient and insentient beings in our heart of unconditional love. When we dwell in no place, that "no place" becomes every place.

Often, we hear spiritual teachers tell us to "be here now!" If we are dwelling in no place, how can we be here now? To further complicate matters, the Diamond Sutra says, "The mind of the future is ungraspable. The mind of the past is ungraspable. The mind of the present is ungraspable."[2] It is easy to understand that the future mind and the past mind are ungraspable. The past mind contains memories of events that are long gone, and our memories do not always reflect what actually happened. The future mind contains our projections about the future, which by definition have not yet occurred. It contains our hopes and our fears, which may or may not play out.

What about the mind of the present? Can't we at least grasp that? The problem is that, as soon as we think we have grasped it, it is already the mind of the past. If we hold on to it, it is no longer the present mind. Since time inexorably moves on, there is no present mind to grasp. This life, this world, is fleeting; time swiftly passes by.

At the end of the Diamond Sutra, the Buddha says to think of this life as "a star at dawn, a bubble on a stream, a flash of lightning in a summer cloud, a flickering lamp, a phantom, and a dream."[3]

"Dwelling in no place, raise the Bodhi mind." This profound line has reverberated throughout the Zen tradition. In the year 660, while carrying wood in the marketplace, Huineng, the future Sixth Zen Ancestor who we met in a previous chapter, heard a monk chanting that line. Huineng had a spontaneous deep realization, which is quite remarkable given that he is commonly thought to have been an illiterate wood gatherer trying to survive with his widowed mother. Despite his great awakening experience, Huineng was not satisfied and told himself, "I seek the Great Teaching, why should I stop halfway?" Perhaps he understood that even seeing deeply into emptiness did not mean he would be able to put it into practice in his daily life.

Logic cannot resolve this issue or even really reach it, because in logic we manipulate thought objects and try to give them some reality to which we can grab. Because we have not developed confidence and trust in ourselves, we continue to look for a flash of insight or sign outside ourselves rather than shedding the skin of our old habit-ridden selves and entering the unknown.

In this unknown realm, we cannot rely on any of our old tricks for maintaining separation, which is the actual cause of our confusion. When we let go of the small, separate self, we can rest in the bosom of True Self. When we fully accept all reality just as it is, the struggle is over. That acceptance includes compassion for ourselves just as we are. It is a deep surrender of the whole being to the simple truth of all-embracing love.

Dwelling in no place and surrendering to the unknown means being free in every situation in life. It means not being constrained by former opinions and ideas. It means being able to flow according to the circumstances that present themselves. The circumstances always depend on the time, place, people involved, and intensity of the situation. Being able to adapt without holding on to fixed opinions is the mark of the person who is dwelling in no place.

This wisdom, the wisdom of the third rank, is known as the Marvelous Observing Wisdom, or the Wisdom of Discernment. Let's look at a koan that illustrates it.

Priest Taigen of Sogen Temple in Japan's Bizen Province did *saisan* (further studies), visiting Priest Gyoo in Yoshu Province. When Taigen was about to leave, Gyoo said, "Since I have nothing to give you, I should like to make this as my present." Then he picked up a burning piece of charcoal from the hearth with the fire tongs and gave it to Taigen.

Taigen did not know how to receive it. He stamped out of the room and locked himself in one of the rooms there for seven days. Taigen went to see Gyoo again to say goodbye, only to have Gyoo offer him a burning charcoal once again. This time, however, Taigen had no hesitation in taking care of the matter. Gyoo approved it.[4]

Taigen could not be ungrateful and refuse the "present," nor could he receive it without burning himself. What did he do?

When you are challenged, you can defend or you can dance. We all know about being defensive, but how about dancing? The readiness to dance frees you from your karma. Sometimes we think that we are dancing when we are really stepping on the toes of our partner. A verse of *The Song of the Jewel Mirror Samadhi* states, "The wooden man starts to sing, the stone woman gets up dancing."

That is real freedom. For another instance of it, consider

the relationship between Isan and Ryutetsuma (Ch. Liu Tiemo) as described in case 60 of *The Book of Equanimity*. Ryutetsuma was a Zen nun who built a hut just outside of Isan's monastery and studied with him and other Zen masters when she could. They called her Iron Grinder Liu because she could defeat all of the monks in Dharma combat. She ground up even the most combative monks. Isan and Ryutetsuma had a close, familiar relationship.

One day, Ryutetsuma arrived at Isan's place, and Isan said, "Old cow, you've come!" ("Old cow" is a reference to the ox or True Self.)

Ryutetsuma said, "There's a big feast on Mount Tai tomorrow, Osho. Are you going?"

Isan lay himself down. At that, Ryutetsuma left.

Mount Tai was many days' walk from Isan's place. Ryutetsuma's invitation is like me asking you to join me for a picnic on the moon. No wonder Isan lay down. He found Mount Tai in his bed without taking an arduous journey. Ryutetsuma responded, "Okay, if that is the way you feel about it," and she waltzed away.

What a wonderful dance between two old friends.

Hard though it may be in the midst of nothing,
there is a way free from dust.

This first line of Tozan's verse for the third rank teaches that you are always fundamentally aware of the empty nature of everything that arises. How do you not fall into the traps of life, the slings and arrows of outrageous fortune? Let's look at some examples from the tradition.

Bankei (1622–1693) was a seventeenth-century Zen master in Japan. Once, a neighboring priest scolded his students for abandoning his school to study with Bankei instead. He yelled at Bankei and tried to one-up him by saying that his teacher could perform miracles, such as walking on water and signing his name from the other side of a river. Bankei replied, "My miracle is that when I'm hungry, I eat, and when I am tired, I sleep."[5] Bankei was, in fact, borrowing this wise response from an older Zen source.

Dazhu Huihai (d. 788) was asked by a Vinaya master (a master of Buddhist monastic rules and ethics), "When one seeks to follow the Way, is there a particular manner in which he should behave?"

"There is," Dazhu said.

"Please tell me about it," the Vinaya master requested.

"When one is hungry, one eats; when one is tired, one sleeps."

"But everyone does that," the Vinaya master complained. "Your behavior isn't different from that of commoners."

"They're not the same at all," Dazhu said.

"In what way are they different?"

"When most people eat, they don't just eat; their minds are preoccupied with a thousand different fantasies. When they sleep, they don't just sleep; their minds are filled with any number of idle thoughts."[6]

In *The Song of the Jewel Mirror Samadhi*, which is considered to be a precursor to the Five Ranks of Tozan, the last lines are as follows:

Ministers serve their lords, children obey their
parents.
Not obeying is not filial, failure to serve is no help.
Practicing unobserved, functioning secretly, like a
fool, like an idiot.
Just to continue in this way is called the host within
the host.

Ministers and their lords, and children and their parents,
could be metaphors for the relative and the absolute. Things
need to be in order or there is chaos. If children do not follow
the directions of their parents, then they are not acting like
children. If a minister does not serve his lord, it not only does
not help but might also lead to corporal punishment. These
examples are drawn from Chinese standards of a thousand
years ago, but for our purposes, they mean that if our relative
actions are not in accord with the essence of the absolute,
then we give rise to suffering. When we do practice skillfully,
it is unobserved and functions secretly—like a fool, like an
idiot, like an old ignorant woman finding her ancient mirror.

Practicing unobserved and functioning secretly is considered a high state of spiritual realization in the Zen tradition—and in some parts of contemporary culture too. As the
bumper sticker says, "Practice random acts of kindness." Or
as the anonymous saying goes, "There is no limit to what
you can accomplish if you do not care who gets the credit."

After I lived in the monastic community at the Zen Center of Los Angeles as a monk, I went back to the workforce

and got a job as a software engineer in the factory automation and control business. I quickly was moved to a middle management position, and I was never afraid to hire people smarter than I was. I always strived to make my managers look good by getting projects done well and in a timely manner. I knew how to manage up and how to manage down. I made sure that my employees had the tools and training they needed to do a good job. In some situations, I was the lord and in others, the minister. And without promoting myself, I just kept getting promoted. Both my managers and my employees trusted me.

I took this smooth career progress as evidence of what I'd absorbed in my Zen training. Namely that, as situations change, we need to adjust or things can fall apart. I had also learned so much from my time at the Zen center about simply proceeding with awareness amid ordinariness. In the midst of nothing, when the bell strikes, we go to the meditation hall. When the alarm clock rings, we get out of bed. If there is no hesitation, no equivocation, no resistance, that is a way to be free from dust.

There is another miscellaneous koan that speaks to this first line of Tozan's verse on the third rank. The koan goes, "Empty-handed yet holding a hoe." This is like playing a guitar without using your hands or singing a song without using your voice. If you are skilled and totally engaged without thinking, you can do it. You forget your hands, and you just play. You forget your voice, and you just sing. In the midst of nothing, you forget yourself and are free.

The following anecdote comes from case 89 of *The Book of Equanimity*.

Attention! Tozan addressed the assembly, saying, "Beginning autumn at summer's end, my brothers, some of you will go east and some west. But straightaway go to a place where there is no grass for a thousand miles."

Then he added, "But as in a place where there is no grass for a thousand miles, how can you go?"

Sekiso (Ch. Shishuang Qingzhu) said, "Go out the gate, and there's grass."

Taiyo (Ch. Dayang Jingxuan) then said, "Don't go out the gate, and there's grass all over everywhere."

For the Chinese and Japanese, grass is a weed. If you go to Japan, you will see that they pull up all the grass in most of the beautiful gardens. It's just gravel and rocks and trees, bushes and moss, that remain. No grass means no weeds, no delusions, and no attachments. One thousand miles means everywhere. If you go outside the gate, there's grass, and if you don't go outside the gate, there's grass. Wherever you go, there is always grass. So, what are you going to do?

The point of this koan is to be at home in any situation and remain undisturbed inside and outside. Here, *outside* means seeing the true nature of phenomena without adding anything extra; *inside* means seeing the true nature of one's self without sprouting weeds and grass.

Master Baso (Ch. Mazu Daoyi) said that this very mind is Buddha. It's our everyday mind—the mind with which we wake up, the mind with which we go to the bathroom, the mind with which we eat our breakfast, the mind with which we walk to the zendo, the mind with which we sit down, the mind with which we practice zazen, the mind with which we go to work. When we try to describe it, it becomes elusive because this mind that is Buddha comes out of our own experience. As soon as we describe it, there are grasses everywhere.

Master Keizan wrote this poem for the case of the Fortieth Ancestor in *The Transmission of Light*:

> Seeking it oneself with empty hands,
> You return with empty hands;
> In that place where fundamentally nothing
>   is acquired,
> You really acquire it.

Today's ability to avoid the forbidden name

What is the forbidden name? In ancient China, the name of the emperor could not be spoken. In some theistic traditions, the name of God cannot be spoken or written. In Buddhism, synonyms for God could be "True Nature," "True Self," "the Absolute," "Thusness," or "Suchness." If one mentions it as if it were an object to understand, right there it is missed. So, this line is telling us not to even raise the thought of "*my* true self."

Case 48 of *The Book of Equanimity* presents a part of the Vimalakirti Sutra in which the bodhisattva Vimalakirti questioned numerous other bodhisattvas about entering the nondual Dharma gate. At a certain point, he got to question the Great Wisdom bodhisattva Manjushri, asking, "What about a bodhisattva entering the nondual Dharma gate?"

Manjushri replied, "As I understand it, with regard to all dharmas, there are no words or speech, no revelation or knowledge, and it is separate from all conversation. This is entering the nondual Dharma gate."

Thereupon, Manjushri questioned Vimalakirti, saying, "All of us bodhisattvas have each had our say, Venerable Sir, now you should expound about a bodhisattva entering the nondual Dharma gate."

Vimalakirti maintained silence.

Vimalakirti's response is called his "thunderous silence." It shakes heaven and earth and avoids the forbidden name.

In koans, we can find more examples of practitioners avoiding the forbidden name.

In case 70 of *The Blue Cliff Record*, Hyakujo (Ch. Baizhang Huaihai) asked, "How do you speak with your mouth shut?"

Isan replied, "I ask you to speak instead, Teacher."

Hyakujo said, "It's not that I refuse to tell you, but I'm afraid that afterward I would be bereft of descendants."

Isan spoke and did not get trapped by Hyakujo's question. Hyakujo's final reply is what we call praising by slander. They both avoided getting trapped and thus avoided the forbidden name.

In case 39 of *The Book of Equanimity*, a monk said to Joshu, "Your student has just entered the monastery. Please, Master, instruct me."

Joshu said, "Did you finish your rice gruel?"

The monk replied, "I have finished eating."

Joshu remarked, "Then wash your bowls."

On one level, this koan is about taking care of the details of your life. Those of you who cook for your family know that the meal is over only after the kitchen is clean—not after the last bite is eaten. We leave a lot of things half-done. In the preface to this case, it says, "When food comes, stuff the mouth. When sleep comes, close the eyes." When you eat, there is nothing in the universe but eating. It consumes heaven and earth. When we clean, we clean. But there's also more going on in this koan.

The monk says, "Instruct me," and Joshu asks, "Have you finished your rice gruel?" Another way of hearing this question is as "Have you accomplished anything at all?" Then the monk answers, "Yes, I have," and Joshu responds, "Well, then wash it away. Don't hold on to it."

Joshu is telling the monk not to cling to anything, least of all transcendent experiences. They will cause your life to stagnate faster than anything else. Anything we hold on to can become the forbidden name. Avoid it.

Surpasses yesterday's most eloquent discussion.

A Chinese proverb says, "Having nothing is better than having something good." Avoiding the forbidden name is better than describing it in the most eloquent discussion. Don't add anything extra, and then nothing can defeat you. Even buddhas and patriarchs cannot top you.

Many of the eloquent discussions of Western philosophy try to describe the forbidden name rather than avoiding the futility of adding unnecessary complications. The eighteenth-century Scottish philosopher David Hume wrote:

> For my part when I enter most intimately into what
> I call myself I always stumble on some particular
> perception or other, of heat or cold, light or shade,
> love or hatred, pain or pleasure, I never can catch
> myself at any time without a perception, and never
> can observe anything but the perception.[7]

I would ask him, "Who is it who perceives the 'perception'?" Hume never figured it out. He was resigned to accepting a separation between his philosophy and his life. He retired to play backgammon.

Immanuel Kant, the eighteenth-century German philosopher, reacting to Hume, wrote that there is a self, but we can never know it: "No fixed and abiding self can present itself in this flux of inner perceptions. . . . Therefore there must be a condition that precedes all experience and which makes experience itself possible."[8]

Kant thus created a new ephemeral entity to call the self. He called it transcendental apperception, which means "beyond introspective self-consciousness."

These philosophers made most eloquent discussions about identifying the self and kept coming up with contradictions that required them to invent something that could not be experienced. Zen does not depend upon words and letters. It is a transmission outside the scriptures and points directly to one's heart.

The famous Nobel physicist Erwin Schrödinger became interested in philosophy late in his career. He was particularly intrigued by the question "What is the self?" He came to this conclusion, which could be part of a Buddhist sutra:

> The reason why our sentient, percipient and thinking ego is met nowhere within our scientific world picture can be easily indicated in seven words, *because it is itself the world picture* [emphasis added]. It is identical with the whole and therefore cannot be contained in it as part of it. [9]

What surpasses all of these eloquent discussions? *The Book of Equanimity* case 46 shows how to avoid the forbidden name and surpass eloquent discussion: Attention! Great Master Emmyo Tokusan (Ch. Deshan Yuanmi) addressed the assembly, saying, "Exhaust the end and there's instant attainment. The mouths of all Buddhas of the three times might as well hang upon the wall. Now, there's a person who roars with laughter. Ha! Ha! When you know this one, the essence of your exhaustive study is completed."

As recorded in Dogen's *Eihei Koroku*, Dogen's teacher, Tendo Nyojo, said, "The entire body is a mouth hanging in the air."[10] When Tokusan says that the mouths of all the buddhas of the three times might as well hang on the wall, he's saying even the buddhas can't express this exhausted end. When Tendo Nyojo says the entire body is a mouth hanging in the air, he's saying, "You're expressing it all the time." It cannot be expressed, and yet you're expressing it all the time. As soon as you think you've grabbed it, it has moved. Yet you're constantly expressing it. Why? Tokusan says, "There's a person who roars with laughter," and then he laughs. "Ha! Ha! When you know this one, the essence of your exhaustive study is completed."

When the entire body and mind are watching a movie, the movie is watching the movie. The entire body and mind are a mouth hanging in the air. When you speak, use your whole body and mind. If your body and mind are the entire body and mind hanging in space, they are the body and mind of the universal emptiness. If not, it's just some kind of an idea, some kind of concept, a false basis that depends on your own image of who you are.

The third rank emphasizes penetrating into the absolute but not dwelling there as if in an ice cave. Here, you let your situation enter you fully, whether it be bereavement, joy, or danger. If you allow the afflictions to advance and confirm you, your body and mind drop off, and the birds are chirping.

The point in this rank is to bring forth the heart of the fathomless void and present the appropriate topic clearly or take the appropriate action decisively. Zen Master Kozan Ichikyo wrote the following poem at the end of his life:[11]

Empty-handed I entered the world.
Barefoot I leave it.
My coming, my going—
Two simple happenings
That got entangled.

Our lives are one long entangled vine. How can we be free from entanglements? You know the answer. Be entangled.

o o o o o

PRACTICE QUESTION

In your active, arduous life, how do you find a way free from dust?

6

Fourth Hensho Goi

Reaching in the Midst of the Relative

THE SEEMING UNITING WITH THE REAL
There is no need to avoid crossed swords
A good hand, like a lotus blooming in a fire
Can leap right through the sky.

> (Luk, *Ch'an and Zen Teaching*)

GOING WITHIN TOGETHER
Crossed swords, neither permitting retreat;
Dexterously wielded, like a lotus amidst fire,
Similarly, there is a natural determination to ascend
the heavens.

> (Powell, *The Record of Tung-shan*)

PROCEEDING WITHIN PHENOMENA
Like two crossed swords, neither permitting retreat;
Dexterously wielded, like the lotus in the midst
of fire—
A natural imperative to assail heaven itself.

> (Aitken, *The Morning Star*)

THE ARRIVAL AT MUTUAL INTEGRATION

When two blades cross points, there is no need to
   withdraw,
The master swordsman is like the lotus blooming
   in the fire.
Such a man has in and of himself a heaven-soaring
   spirit.

(Miura and Sasaki, Zen Dust)

To ATTAIN the fourth rank is to have reached the stage where mountains really are mountains, and you have fully integrated the nature of mountains into your being. You will understand when you penetrate the koan, "Create a mountain." Likewise, if you penetrate the miscellaneous koan where a monk asked Ummon, "How do buddhas appear?" Ummon replied, "The eastern mountain walks along the stream."

There is nothing hidden. If you do not see it, you do not see it even as you walk on it. Or, in Ummon's case, if you do not see the eastern mountain, you do not see it even as you walk *as* it. You are the eastern mountain that walks along the stream. How would you present it?

In this rank, you see that your Buddha Nature is everything, and everything is your Buddha Nature in you.

Let's examine the following koan.

A monk asked Master Joshu, "What is the meaning of Bodhidharma coming from the West?"

Joshu answered, "The cypress tree in the garden." (*Gateless Gate*, case 37 and *Book of Equanimity*, case 47).

The question can be interpreted as "What is Zen?" or even "What is the meaning of my life?" The cypress tree in the garden!

One blossom bespeaks of a boundless spring. One drop bespeaks the ocean's water. The cypress tree in the garden bespeaks heaven and hell, the Great Earth, the moon, the sun, the planets, and all the stars.

Dogen relates the remainder of this koan in *Shobogenzo*, "Hakujushi" ("The Oak Tree"):

The monk then said to Joshu, "You should not give such an objective answer."

Joshu replied, "I didn't."

Then the monk asked again, "What is the meaning of Bodhidharma coming from the West?"

Joshu answered, "The cypress tree in the garden."

Most people do not see the cypress tree in the garden because they are looking for something marvelous or magical to confirm that the transcendent is beyond the subtle manifestation of daily life. That is the ego-grasping mind full of concepts and always looking for something outside itself.

Since there is no subjectivity or objectivity in the cypress tree in the garden, it is rooted in complete freedom. Isn't its sheer existence marvelous and magical enough?

The spiritual process is a literal stripping away of all the layers of falsity and illusion that cover, distort, and hide our understanding. We don't discover Truth or God somewhere outside ourselves; rather, we uncover it within.

There is a story about a *tenzo* (head cook at a Zen monastery) that illustrates the effortless compassion of this fourth rank:

At the monastery of Fugai Ekun, ceremonies delayed
preparation of the noon meal one day, and when
they were over, the cook took up his sickle and hur-

riedly gathered up vegetables from the garden. In his haste he lopped off part of a snake, and unaware that he had done so, threw it in the soup pot with the vegetables.

At the meal, the monks thought that they had never tasted such a delicious soup, but the Roshi found something remarkable in his bowl. Summoning the cook, he held up the head of a snake and demanded, "What is this?"

The cook took the morsel, saying, "Oh, thank you, Roshi," and immediately ate it.[1]

This dialogue is called "Eating the Blame," and it shows how to use a challenge and not be used by it. The cook had nothing to defend. He did not have to make excuses, and he did not take the roshi's challenge as an accusation. He took the matter in hand and gave everyone a wonderful *teisho* (Dharma talk). That is what our Zen training is about. Be aware of your position and your responsibilities. When you embody this rank, you can begin to genuinely assist sentient beings to realize their own Buddha Nature. "Reaching in the midst of the relative" is about right understanding and right action.

Here again is Tozan's verse for this rank:

There is no need to avoid crossed swords
A good hand, like a lotus blooming in a fire
Has in itself a heaven-soaring spirit.

There is no need to avoid crossed swords

The soul that is truly committed to awakening does not flee uncomfortable situations until it believes that it has fully extracted all the wisdom it can.

Ultimately, to awaken completely requires the dismantling of the very subtle, deeply embedded patterns of false perception you've developed in this life. The slate must be wiped clean so all that remains is the reality of life, with no filament or trace of egoic consciousness left.

That is not an easy thing to do, yet it requires no effort, save the effort to manifest as unconditional love—first for yourself, then extending to others. It is a deep commitment to stay present to that love in all conditions and all circumstances.

In the Gnostic Gospels, Jesus is quoted as saying, "If you bring forth what is in you, what you bring forth will save you. If you do not bring forth what is within you, what you do not bring forth will kill you."[2]

If you suppress your discomfort and leave it buried, it will come back and bite you. By opening yourself up to your indecision and dread, you will find the freedom that has been eluding you. That is the spirit of this fourth rank.

I heard a story about a Thai Theravadan monk who felt aroused whenever he saw a young woman who served the monks in the temple. He would meditate and try to quiet his mind and emotions, but to no avail. Finally, he told himself that he could not control his attraction to the young woman, so he would have to kill himself rather than break his monk's vows. Of course, one of the vows is to not take life, including one's own. Fortunately, an older monk sensed

his anguish and arranged to have the young woman trans-
ferred to another temple to fulfill her tasks of service to
the ordained monks. It is a pity that the unfortunate young
woman had to be a pawn in this drama and had no say in
her assignment.

This monk did not know that you can have feelings and
not be compelled to act on them. As the verse says, "There is
no need to avoid crossed swords." There is no need to avoid
all the conflicts and confusion that arise in your life. Why?
Because at this stage in your practice, you know how to
deal with difficulties. How can you approach disagreements
without falling into duality?

One can think about the crossed swords in terms of the
absolute and the relative. In this fourth stage, there is no
duality. "Reaching in the midst of the relative," or "the relative uniting with the absolute," implies that one lives in the
relative world and functions from the absolute. The relative
is united with the absolute. Thus, there is no duality. Don't
create it!

The famous koan of Nansen and the cat is a classic example of not avoiding crossed swords.

At Nansen's place one day, the monks of the East and
West Halls were arguing about a cat. Seeing this, Nansen
held it up before him, saying, "If you can say a word, I won't
cut it." The assembly made no response. Nansen cut the cat
in two. (*Book of Equanimity*, case 9; *Blue Cliff Record*, case 63;
Gateless Gate, case 14)

This case is both famous and controversial. When Zen
students first hear it, they wonder how a Zen master could

take the life of a living being, especially given the Buddhist precept of not taking but cherishing life. Of course, in the history of Zen, there are lots of cases of Zen masters hitting their students and shouting at them as ways of exhorting them to realize their true selves. I taught classes on Zen Buddhism at Naropa University, and a lot of the students from Buddhist sects other than Zen would say, "Why is Zen so cruel?" When I talked about this case, it just reaffirmed for them that Zen is cruel. "Why does he have to kill a cat?"

To help answer this question, it's important to know that during the Golden Age of Zen in China (Tang dynasty, circa 800), there was rebellion and famine for many years, and as much as one-third of the Chinese population perished. When nascent Zen masters went on pilgrimage, there were bodies strewn all along the roadsides. So, to spiritually awaken under those kinds of conditions was a very big deal—even the toughest masters might appear like loving grandmas in the conditions they were living through.

Zen is a very disciplined approach to practice. We can waste our time arguing about it, but Zen masters used whatever means were available to bring their students to realization.

I've read commentaries by American Zen teachers on this case that say Nansen really didn't kill a cat, that he only made a gesture, a cutting motion with his hand, like he was going to, but he really didn't do it. They are revisionists! To see this koan clearly, we have to accept that the knife did cut the fur, the skin, the muscle, and the viscera. We don't have to apologize for Nansen. Master Setcho (Ch. Xuetou Chongxian), who compiled *The Blue Cliff Record*, commented on this case, "Fortunately, Nansen took a correct action. Sword straightaway cuts it in two. Criticize as you like."

Nansen is exhorting us to forget the self. Koans do not ignore the rules of moral and ethical behavior, nor do they promote them. The purpose of koans is to liberate us from the suffering caused by moral, ethical, conceptual, and behavioral rules that we use to bind ourselves. Koans teach us to use the rules of behavior to be free and to make lively use of them. Unless we understand this, we cannot understand the koans.

Millions of animals are killed every day, but none of these deaths is a sacrifice for our liberation. Nansen sacrificed the life of one cat for the liberation of hundreds of thousands of beings. He was willing to absorb the negative karma of taking a life in order to liberate his monks.

Due to the psychological and legal landscape of American Zen, it is hard to imagine a present-day roshi cutting a cat in two or even beating a student with a ceremonial stick. We no longer use such aggressive and brutal methods, and such extreme actions are not generally necessary.

In *Shobogenzo*, "Tenzokyokun" ("Instructions to the Head Cook"), Dogen wrote,

> Being scrupulous in our actions and pouring our
> energy into those actions, there is no reason why we
> cannot equal the ancient masters. We must aspire to
> the highest of ideals without becoming arrogant in
> our manner. There, things are truly just a matter of

course. Yet we remain unclear about them because our minds go racing about like horses running wild in the fields, while our emotions remain unmanageable, like monkeys swinging in the trees. If only we would step back to carefully reflect on the horse and monkey, our lives would naturally become one with our work. Doing so is the means whereby we turn things even while simultaneously we are being turned by them. It is vital that we clarify and harmonize our life with our work, and not lose sight of either the absolute or the practical.

"We turn things while we are simultaneously being turned by them" is called the stage of "seamless relationships." Examples are work and practice, partner and partner, mother and child. They can be messy, smooth and seamless, or both—seamless despite inevitable messiness. By being scrupulous in our actions and pouring our energy into those actions, it is possible to realize seamless relationships.

A good hand, like a lotus blooming in a fire

A good hand does not avoid the difficulties of life. Being "selfless," we can act according to our conditions, karma, and vows. When you agree, agree wholeheartedly but don't get stuck in that agreement. When you disagree, disagree wholeheartedly but don't get stuck in that disagreement.

There was a conflict between two members in a spiritual community, and they went before the guru to plead their case. The first person gave their point of view, and the guru said, "You are right!" The second person gave their point of view, and the guru said, "You are right!" Then the guru's attendant asked, "How could you tell the first person, 'You are right' and then tell the second person, 'You are right'?" The guru said, "You are right!"

Who is stuck in agreement? Who is stuck in disagreement?

The image of a lotus blooming in fire is from the Vima-lakirti Sutra: "The lotus blooming in the fire, what a rare occurrence this must be."[3] This is a reference to the bodhi-sattva practicing compassion in the midst of desires.

At the end of the meal, a *gatha* is chanted in many Zen communities. We chant, "May we exist in muddy water with purity like the lotus. Thus we bow to Buddha." The lotus root needs to be in the mud in order to bring forth the exquisite blossom. This is another reference to maintaining one's presence, even in the midst of samsara and suffering.

All of us reach stages in our practice where we hit a wall and darkness descends. There is a natural tendency in Zen centers to want to be the best meditator or the best Zen student. When the luster of that fantasy starts to dim, then the darkness of the unknown begins to descend. Some of us even hit a point of wanting to give up on the spiritual life but find that all alternatives are devoid of any meaning— the darkness descends then, too. At this point, we have no choice but to surrender to the unknown.

"The Dark Night of the Soul" is the title given to two poems written by the sixteenth-century Spanish mystic Saint John of the Cross. The poems narrate the journey of the soul to mystical union with God. The journey is called "the dark night," in part, because darkness represents the fact that the destination—God—is unknowable.

The dark night of the soul has evolved to mean a stage in personal development when a person undergoes a significant transition to a deeper perception of life and their place in it. This enhanced awareness is accompanied by a painful shedding of previous conceptual frameworks, such as an identity, a relationship, a career, a habit, or a belief system, that previously gave them meaning in their life. This line, "a good hand, like a lotus in the fire," points to this kind of transformation.

In her book *The Zen Priestess and the Snake*, Roshi Shinko Perez recalls a devout Catholic aunt telling her that she was going to burn in hell due to something she innocently did as a young child. Shinko believed her aunt and went through the flames of hell, deeply feeling the torment as if she were actually burning up. By surrendering to this fate, Shinko was purified and, like a lotus in the fire, became open to a profound encounter with the Lady of Light, who emanated pure love to this innocent child and impelled her on her spiritual journey.

Another such "dark night" episode occurred when Priest Kato was studying with Kazan Roshi of Iyo in Shikoku. Kazan Roshi was famous for the severity of his training. When Kato and five fellow students went together to Kazan Roshi, he brusquely turned them away, saying, "My temple is too poor to take you in." The students each begged him in turn until he finally said, "Well, then, I'll allow you to come here just to have dokusan with me." The six of them separately found places to stay and had dokusan with him. Kato stayed under the balcony of a shrine in the village.

During the day, the students barely supported themselves by begging for food (*takuhatsu*). Kazan Roshi was moved by the sincere devotion of these monks. He later joined them on takuhatsu so they could receive more offerings and, thus, made it easier for them to pursue their practice.

Now the episode begins: One day, as usual, with Roshi leading the procession, the six students went on takuhatsu. On the way, they came to a road that led up a hill. There was a man pulling a cart so heavily loaded with bundles that he couldn't get it up the hill. Kato automatically left the procession to help the man with his cart. At that instant, Roshi, who normally never turned around, looked at him and suddenly walked back to the temple and told his attendant not to allow Kato to come to the monastery anymore. It was a very heavy punishment—the gravest one. Needless to say, Kato and his friends worried greatly about it and wanted to at least know why he had been expelled. Then Kazan Roshi told them, "Being trainees and on takuhatsu, one's attention should be on takuhatsu, not on another person's situation. That's why I told him to leave."

Having learned the reason, Kato did *monshuku* (an overnight stay before the temple gate) and spent a week doing zazen there while his five Dharma friends continuously begged Roshi to pardon him. Finally, his apology was accepted, and Kato was able to continue dokusan with them again.

Daiun Sogaku Harada Roshi, in whose writings I read this story, concluded with these words: "These monks were as extraordinary as the roshi. Nowadays, how many teachers or monks are such as them? Probably none. To pursue the ordinary practice is not much. However, for those trainees who wish to realize the grave importance of life, their practice must be genuine and undefiled. They must at all times be totally absorbed in their koans wherever they are. When on takuhatsu, to look around is to be distracted. Such a loose attitude is not at all acceptable. Consequently, Kazan Roshi used his killing dagger."[4]

What do you think of this story? On one hand, when I first heard it, I thought it was terrible that Kato would be punished for helping a villager with his cart. On the other hand, the Zen practice of Kazan Roshi required total concentration on one's practice. How does our practice compare? Can we accomplish the fourth rank with half-hearted effort?

This rank emphasizes compassion. It seems obvious that Kato showed his compassion by helping the villager. So, a question arises about the compassion of Kazan Roshi. A case can be made that Kazan Roshi's compassion was the most profound compassion. He made great demands on his students so they could eventually realize their true nature for the sake of all beings. The roshi saw Kato's action as a distraction from a deeper purpose. What do you think?

The Buddhist scholar Francis Dojun Cook wrote,

Shakyamuni Buddha did not dedicate his life simply to helping us to become completely enlightened and to escape the world of karma and rebirth. He taught us, rather, to teach others until such time as the world is full of beings whose sole aim in life is to be of service to others.[5]

A case could be made that Kato was of service to another. A case could also be made that Roshi Kazan was training six monks to be enlightened so they could teach and be of service to others. It is like a pyramid scheme where the students devote their lives to the teachings of the master to pass these teachings on to even more students. The difference here is that everyone reaps the benefits, not just those at the top of the pyramid. Still, you might question Kazan Roshi's methods.

There is a Theravadan story of the Buddha that is like a Zen koan. In that story, a deva asks the Buddha,

"Tell me, dear sir, how you crossed over the flood."

He replies: "I crossed over the flood without pushing forward, without staying in place."

She asks: "But how, dear sir, did you cross over the flood without pushing forward, without staying in place?"

And the Buddha replies: "When I pushed forward, I was whirled about. When I stayed in place, I sank. And so I crossed over the flood without pushing forward, without staying in place."[6]

The Buddha did not answer as the deva expected. So it is in life. If we try to push forward, we find resistance and turbulence; if we try to avoid reality and stand where we already are, we sink into passivity or are overtaken by events. So, how do we manage to get through the flood of life without pushing forward and without staying in place? To do so is to become "a good hand, like a lotus blooming in a fire."

Putting the second and third lines together, we have

> A good hand, like a lotus in the fire,
> Has in itself a heaven-soaring spirit.

Has in itself a heaven-soaring spirit.

You might think that a "heaven-soaring spirit" is a good thing. It is wonderful to be in the company of someone who has such a spirit, but in this rank, it can still be an anchor that prevents one from really soaring. Consider the following story:

Once Nansen (748–835) decided to visit a certain manor house. That night the local God of the Soil informed the lord of the manor that Nansen would come the following morning. So, the lord made preparations. When Nansen arrived, he asked, "How did you know I was coming?"

The manor lord told Nansen that he had been informed by his local god.

Nansen said, "Because this old monk's practice has no power, he is spied upon by gods and demons."

His attendant monk said, "Your reverence, you are already such a good teacher, why should you be spied upon by gods and demons?"

Nansen replied, "Put another portion of food before the local God of the Soil."[7]

A person with a heaven-soaring spirit attracts attention. People notice them. That is why Nansen said that his practice had no power. If he had power, he would be invisible to gods and demons. No one would notice whether he came or went.

One thing I noticed about Maezumi Roshi was that when he entered a room, he found his place in it. He just blended into the environment with no fanfare. In contrast, I once went to see Swami Satchidananda at the invitation of my brother, who was one of his close disciples. We entered the room, and it was adorned with huge, larger-than-life-sized portraits of Swami-ji. There was an ornate chair on a raised platform that towered over the audience. The swami entered to much fanfare. I am not saying that one is better than the other, just that they are different. The Zen way is to go without fanfare.

If someone has truly experienced the fourth rank, how would their life look? Let me give you an example.[8] In ancient China, there was a sage named Gozu Hoyu (Ch. Niutou Farong; 594–657). He was a man of high virtue, and people in his neighborhood respected him deeply. Even birds praised his virtues by fetching flowers and offering them to him. But later on, after he came to great enlightenment under the Fourth Ancestor, Daii Doshin Zenji (Ch. Dayi Daoxin; 580–651), the birds stopped bringing him flowers. As long as people extol you as a great person, a person of high virtue, and so forth, they are putting their projections on you. Their projections are not real. A person of true enlightenment does not look great at all. The birds failed to spot Hoyu Zenji because he turned invisible to them as he became someone who is nowhere.

The accompanying verse from the eighth ox-herding picture (person and ox forgotten) addresses this point: "Holiness, to which birds consecrate flowers, is just a disgrace."[9]

Dogen, in his *Shobogenzo* fascicle "Daigo" ("Great Enlightenment"), wrote,

> Great Enlightenment is the daily activity of the Buddhas and Patriarchs, but they never think about it. Ordinary people cannot grasp this point because they are attached to many things.
>
> You must be completely detached from the notion of Great Enlightenment and never seek or crave it.

Don't make a new resting place of enlightenment. There is no firm ground upon which to stand. There is no fixed truth that we can depend on. How can you function like this?

This quote from Master Rinzai tells us how to function from a groundless place: "Followers of the Way, as to buddhadharma, no effort is necessary. You have only to be ordinary, with nothing to do—defecating, urinating, wearing clothes, eating food, and lying down when tired. Fools laugh at me, But the wise understand."[10]

True heaven-soaring spirit means to act according to conditions, according to your karma. Even when there are difficulties, you are bigger than the situation. Thus, even when you are having difficulties, every day is a good day.

Hakuin commented thus on the fourth Hensho Goi:

Is [the bodhisattva of indomitable spirit] an ordinary
man? Is he a sage? No one can identify him as either
sage or ordinary person. . . . Try to grab his mind
and it is like seeing the horns of a rabbit or grabbing
the hair of a tortoise that has gone beyond the fur-
thest mountain. But this is still not the final attainment. He still holds on to his heaven-soaring spirit.[11]

What is the "heaven-soaring spirit" here? As long as you are
trying to attain something, that is a duality.

We have experientially explored the terrain of the fourth
Hensho rank, where all we can say about the bodhisattva of
indomitable spirit is that they cannot be identified as a sage
or an ordinary person. Yet they sometimes seem to be a sage
and sometimes seem to be ordinary. They are not bright and
shiny, and they have no hooks for others to grab hold of.
Still, they must not consider this state to be their final resting place. What must they do in the end? They must know
that there is one more rank, the rank of "unity attained."

o   o   o   o   o

PRACTICE QUESTION

Do you avoid crossed swords? How? What can you do
differently?

7

Fifth Hensho Goi

Arriving in the Midst of Absolute/Relative (Unity Attained)

INTEGRATION OF THE REAL AND THE SEEMING

Who can be tuned to that beyond what is and what
    is not?
Though all men want to leave the ever-flowing
    stream,
Each is still sitting in darkness black as charcoal.

(Luk, Ch'an and Zen Teaching)

ARRIVING WITHIN TOGETHER

Falling into neither existence nor nonexistence, who
    dares harmonize?
People fully desire to exit the constant flux;
But after bending and fitting, in the end still return
    to sit in the warmth of the coals.

(Powell, The Record of Tung-shan)

ARRIVING WITHIN TOGETHER

Not falling into being or non-being—who can be in
accord with this?
Everyone longs to leave the eternal flux,
Not just to live in harmony, but to return and sit by
the charcoal fire.

(Aitken, *The Morning Star*)

UNITY ATTAINED

Who dares to equal him who falls into neither being
nor non-being?
All men want to leave the current of ordinary life,
But he, after all, comes back to sit among the coals
and ashes.

(Miura and Sasaki, *Zen Dust*)

HAKUIN SAID that to fully appreciate the fifth rank, you need to study the following verse:

> How many times has Tokuun, the idle old gimlet
>   [sharp-witted person],
> Not come down from the Mystic Peak!
> He hires foolish wise men to bring snow
> And he and they together fill up the well.[1]

Here is another translation:

> The lazy Tokuun came down many times
> From the summit of the Mystic Peak.
> Engaging foolish wise men, together
> Filling the well with snow.[2]

The mystic peak of Myobucho is mentioned in the Flower Garland Sutra (Avatamsaka Sutra).[3] Tokuun Zenji dwells on this mystic peak, which is the highest peak of a mountain, representing awakened mind—that absolute place where not even a speck of dust obscures one's vision. Here there's no self or other, not a trace of a person or an animal or an insect. This is the world of our zazen, where there is no self, no hint of anything in the heavens or on earth. This is the state of mind where we lose track of the body, of the zendo, and of this very world. But it is not the same state as depicted in the first rank, because here, Myobucho is present in all activities of the awakened mind. This Myobucho is the source of the wisdom of Manjushri, the bodhisattva of incomparable wisdom.

For the sake of liberating all beings, Tokuun came down off the mountain of form called Myobucho, as it says in the second translation, but everyplace he went, he was still in that Myobucho state of mind. It is a state of pure presence, awareness, devoid of judgments and extraneous thoughts. The ongoing continuation of clear mind moments was all there was. This is the meaning of his never having left the mountain, as it says in the first translation. Whether eating, shitting, or bathing, whether alone or deeply engaged in human relationships, he remained in that place of continuous clear mind moments. In the midst of this awakened mind, he liberated others.

This state of continuous clear mind moments is the satori of everyday life. If we abandon the everyday world, we fall into the realm of nihilism. We can't throw away our lives in the actual world and abandon the liberation of all beings. If we think there's a world separate from the peak of Myobucho, we create a falsehood. Our everyday lives must be the same as Tokuun's stay on Myobucho, never coming down and yet always coming down into everyday life. To abide in the fifth rank, this is how it must be.

At this stage, one has arrived at the total merging of absolute and relative such that not even a trace of absolute or relative remains. Though in former ranks, perceptions of absolute and relative were a skillful means to encourage us to clarify different aspects of reality, when we have reached this rank, such artificial designations are no longer necessary.

Each of our lives is whole and complete, and when we realize that truth, there is no need to analyze it into categories. We just need to live it, serving all those who need our service.

"Filling the well with snow"—what does this line from Hakuin mean? As much as you try, you can never fill up the well with snow. It is a reference to our bodhisattva vows, which are never ending. We don't take action because we expect a certain result; we do it because it needs to be done. We pick up the shovel, not because we're going to fill the well with snow but because shoveling is the Dharma activity of that moment. We show up for the impossible: saving all beings when there is no one to save.

Here is a description of the state represented by the tenth ox-herding picture, which is the final stage in that traditional Zen representation of the path:

> Whoever has brought the experience of truth to completion in himself goes into the world to liberate others. He immerses and concentrates himself in liberating. All Buddhas and masters have done this since ancient times. Out of the boundless compassion that springs forth he throws himself into the dusty world and, with his great vow, turns his hand to liberating all worldly beings. Can his behavior be described as moral or religious? No, neither the one nor the other. His doing and the unhindered life of Zen which flows in it cannot be pressed into the framework of ethics or religion. No one can render the free play of his life intellectually comprehensible; it is beyond laws or

rules. It is actually this freely playing life that all moral laws and religious rules spring from in the first place.

He appears in the realm of the Buddha, the realm of hell and in worldly passions and wisdom at will. He buries his illuminated nature and visits the wine shops and fish stalls to awaken the drunkards there to themselves. This is the self-immersing and self-concentrating in the play of the original self.[4]

Tozan's verse for this rank is:

Who can be tuned to that beyond what is and what
is not?
Though everyone wants to leave the ever-flowing
stream,
Each is still sitting in darkness black as charcoal.

Who can be tuned to that beyond what is and what is not?

A line in *Trust in Heart/Mind* says, "What is is not and what is not is." What is not?

There is a story of a man who lived near a military base. Every morning, they fired off the cannon at 6 a.m. He was so used to it that he slept right through the noise. One morning the gun malfunctioned and did not fire. At 6 a.m. the man jumped up in bed and said, "What's that?" The absence of the usual sound functioned like something existent to the man, so "what is not" is.

When everything is functioning smoothly, you don't notice it. You don't notice how your heart or your kidneys function unless they are in distress. I read that there are a billion billion billion atoms in my body, bundled into about thirty-seven trillion cells that do all the work of keeping me alive and conscious. There could be as many as a million trillion chemical reactions happening every second in each of the thirty-seven trillion cells that are me. How is it possible to keep track of so much happening so fast, and all of it subject to quantum mechanics—the house rules of the extremely small? It's not surprising that I can't consciously know what is and what is not.

Great Master Ummon said, "Between Heaven and Earth, within the universe, there is one treasure, secretly dwelling in the mountainous shape." (*Book of Equanimity*, case 92) This jewel is secretly dwelling in the mountain shape, which is nothing but your own body. It's dwelling secretly because if you try to look directly at it, you can't see it. And its function is a dark mystery because no matter how hard you try, you cannot fathom how it functions. The eye can't see the eye. This one treasure does not recognize the one treasure. So, how can we fathom it?

You don't notice how this one treasure functions unless you are attached to right and wrong. Then it becomes something other than the one treasure.

When I was working as an oceanographer, we would put instrumented buoys out in the ocean to monitor the environment. Two main hazards would cause the buoys to break free and drift: harsh weather would cause huge waves to rip out the moorings, and sharks would bite the mooring lines. Sometimes the mooring line would be several miles long.

It was always a pity when a shark nipped the line and set the buoy adrift with all of its expensive instruments. One clever oceanographer discovered that sharks would not disturb the lines if they were seamless. To an oceanographer, a seamless mooring line would have no gradations or variations. If you had to stitch two pieces of line together, you'd have to make it look like one line with no joints. To a shark, which only attends to discontinuities or gaps in the fabric of the line, a seamless mooring line looks like nothing—or at least nothing worth biting. What is is not.

If you're steady, consistent, and uniform in your practice, you become seamless (and invulnerable to shark attacks)! There are no indications of unevenness, no gaps, no inside or outside.

That is "what is not." Now, what is?

There is a story about a young monk whose master announced that his protégé had reached an advanced state of enlightenment. The news caused some stir. Some of the monks went to see the young monk.

"We heard you are enlightened. Is that true?" they asked.

"I guess it is," he replied.

"And how do you feel?" they asked.

"As miserable as ever," said the monk.

This is an example of "what is."

Having an awakening experience does not suddenly make you happy forever. Nor does it suddenly make you a better basketball player. It's just what is.

Anything that arises in the realm of human perception falls into the category of what is. When it elicits strong feelings, it stands out in our experience. Strong feelings can originate from just about anything, like the following examples.

Beethoven's "Ode to Joy" in his Ninth Symphony is exquisite and beautiful. It brings much joy to those who hear it. It is an example of what is.

The famous catch by Willie Mays during the 1954 World Series is another example of what is. The Say Hey Kid made an incredible over-the-shoulder catch of a towering drive by Vic Wertz to deep center field. It brought joy to Giants fans and misery to Indians fans. And it brought awe to everyone.

There is a cycle of is and is not for everything. Thoughts arise, exist, and decay. As does everything else. If we try to grab one part of the cycle, it changes immediately. Thus, what is is not and what is not is.

How can we be tuned to that beyond what is and what is not? How do we leave the eternal cycle?

In case 43 of The Gateless Gate, Master Shuzan (Ch. Shoushan Xingnian) held up a shippei (a Zen ceremonial staff) before his disciples and said, "If you call this a shippei, you oppose its reality. If you do not call this a shippei, you deny the fact. Now tell me, what will you call it?

Then Mumon (Ch. Wumen Huikai) said, "You should not use words. You should not use no-words. Speak at once! Speak at once!"

Can you be tuned to that which is beyond what is and what is not? If you call it a shippei, you are stuck in that position. If you avoid calling it a shippei, then you are retreating into an ice cave. Without falling to one side or the other, how can you acknowledge the shippei prior to using words and prior to avoiding words? If you hesitate, the master will strike you with the shippei.

In *Trust in Heart/Mind*, it says,

> Seek movement and there's no-movement, seek rest and no-rest comes instead.
> When rest and no-rest cease to be, then even oneness disappears.

When oneness disappears, what is the shippei?

As I mentioned in chapter 1, in twentieth-century physics there was a big debate about whether electrons and other elementary particles are particles or waves. Sometimes they act like waves, and sometimes they behave as particles. The brilliant Nobel physicist Richard Feynman said that they are neither waves nor particles, but they are something else. The "something else" cannot be known.

Trust in Heart/Mind says, "Awakening is to go beyond emptiness as well as form."

What is it that is beyond both emptiness and form? Like the particle/wave debate, we can't say definitively what it is.

Who can be attuned to that which is beyond what is and what is not? Awakening is to go beyond both emptiness and form. Then what is it?

It is neither absolute nor relative. It is something else that we can never know. Roshi Bernie Glassman said that the purpose of Zen is to realize the oneness and interdependence of life. What is beyond being and nonbeing is life itself. Bernie called this fifth rank "Bearing Witness to Life." What is life? It can be experienced, but it cannot be pinned down intellectually.

Again, from *Trust in Heart/Mind* comes this advice: "Cut off all useless thought and words and there is nowhere you cannot go."

Our useless thoughts and words are what keep us from "going" into the heart of the matter, which is none other than our own lives, utterly transformed, yet at the same time just as it is and always was. As Maezumi Roshi said, "You are always living your life, so you might as well appreciate it."

Though everyone wants to leave the ever-flowing stream,

There can be two interpretations to this line: Everyone wants to accomplish themselves further, or everyone wants to leave the realm of suffering. Ultimately, these two interpretations merge since each is informed by the other.

Hermann Hesse's novel *Siddhartha* is about the spiritual journey of a man by that name, which also is the name of the historical Buddha. The protagonist becomes enlightened by listening to the voice of the river. Rather than leaving the ever-flowing stream, Siddhartha becomes one with it. When he becomes one with the stream, all distinctions between him and the stream vanish, and in a sense, both disappear. Since they have disappeared, we can say that he has left the ever-flowing stream. There is just the flow. The events in our lives flow from one to the next. Our awareness of self flows from one moment to the next, and we conclude that the self persists from each moment to the next. This is false understanding. No matter how hard you look, you will not find a self. Nonetheless, there is flowing.

Siddhartha watches the crystal movement of the water, and the voice within him is strong and loving. He knows that the person who has grasped the secrets of the river must know many other things. One of these secrets is the water's constancy—it is always running but never runs out. Siddhartha does not fully understand this secret but knows that it is special. But what he learns most from the river is how to listen with an open heart.[5]

The river has taught Siddhartha that the source occurs at the same moment as the end. There is no separation from one end of the river to the other. He learns to see his own life this way; from his birth to his death, all is one whole. He sees the world as a river, the wholeness of the river is the wholeness of the world, and now the voice comes to him in a single word. Hesse uses the word *om*; Zen Buddhists use the word *mu*.

The Buddha's quest was to leave the ever-flowing stream of suffering due to birth, sickness, old age, and death. He grew up in a palace with all the comforts that wealth could afford. Yet when he encountered suffering in the world, he felt compelled to begin an endless journey to understand its causes and cessation. As Shakyamuni Gautama, he practiced as an ascetic for six years and was not satisfied. He did not escape the ever-flowing stream of suffering. It was when he took nourishment and sat under the Bodhi tree for seven days and seven nights that he was awakened by seeing the morning star at the end of the last night. He became the Buddha, the Awakened One, and he realized the fulfillment of his quest. When the Buddha started to teach, his first teaching was the Four Noble Truths, which articulated the cause of suffering and the means by which one can leave the ever-flowing stream of suffering.

The Buddha said, "The life of mortals in this world is troubled and brief and combined with pain. For there is not any means by which those that have been born can avoid dying; after reaching old age there is death; of such a nature are living beings. As ripe fruits are early in danger of falling, so mortals when born are always in danger of death. As all earthen vessels made by the potter end in being broken, so is the life of mortals. Both young and adult, both those who are fools and those who are wise, all fall into the power of death; all are subject to death."[6]

This is our karma, and it is this fact that brings many people to practice. We all want to leave the stream of suffering. Far beyond deluded thought, this is nirvana. Deluded thoughts are dualistic thoughts of creating a division between ourselves and others, whether other people or other things. When we have no separation between ourselves and the ever-flowing stream, this is nirvana.

A monk asked Tozan, "Among the three bodies, which one does not fall into any numbers?"

Tozan replied, "As to this, I always take heed." (*Book of Equanimity*, case 98)

Here is an accomplished Zen master who does not rest on his laurels. To him, to leave the ever-flowing stream means to always take heed. What is that *always* referring to? It doesn't mean I take heed when I feel good. It doesn't mean I take heed when I have had enough sleep. It doesn't mean I take heed when I feel like it. It means *always!* In *Eihei Koroku*, Dogen said that our practice is like rubbing sticks together to create a fire.[7] When it starts to get hot, if you decide, "Hey, I think I'll not pay heed for a while," what happens to the fire? Always take heed.

A well-known Buddhist saying states, "If you want to know the causes of the past, look at the effects in the present. If you want to know what the future effects are going to be, look at the present causes." Makes sense, doesn't it? It even says that in the Bible: "If you sow the wind, you'll reap the whirlwind." (Hosea 8:7) It's obvious. Everything we do, everything we say, everything we think has consequences. So, pay heed! According to the Mahaparinibbana Sutta, the Buddha's last words were, "Tread the path with care."

American culture has long upheld a romantic notion of rugged individualism, but there is no such thing as a "self-made man." Everyone depends on others for whatever they achieve in life. The wealthy depend on those who do the hard work to maintain their wealth and position.

Before every meal at the Zen center, we chant, "Seventy-two labors brought us this food, we should know how it comes to us." This refers to the seventy-two positions in a traditional Zen monastery in China and Japan. These include workers in the fields, cooks, servers, administrators, buyers, teachers, cleaners, and so on. Think of how many hands the food at the grocery store passes through before it gets to you.

We are all inextricably bound together, such that whatever you do affects me, and whatever I do affects you. We all "co-arise," and life is thoroughly relational.

Indeed, everything appears to be thoroughly relational. The 2022 Nobel Prize in Physics went to three physicists who articulated quantum entanglement, which basically states that no object can exist independently from other objects. All objects are entangled, and none have an independent existence with definite properties of their own. Instead, they only exist in relation to other objects. We Buddhists use the phrase "codependent origination" or Thich Nhat Hahn's word *interbeing* to describe this.

Many indigenous cultures and Goddess religions intimately know about our interconnectedness. The Mother Goddess connects us all to the sacred. Many ancient societies saw the planet and all life as sacred. Family was sacred, the earth was sacred, and all life had meaning in our interconnectedness in the sacred circle of oneness.

In August 2015, I spent five days camping in the Black Hills of South Dakota at a Lakota Sioux ceremonial site. I was there as part of a Zen Peacemaker Bearing Witness retreat to bear witness to the stories of Native Americans in the area, to visit their Pine Ridge reservation and the Wounded Knee memorial, and to share their ceremonies.

I deeply resonated with the Native Americans' respect for Mother Earth. The first morning, as every morning, we did a sunrise ceremony. We formed a circle, and all the Native Americans stood at the east gate while a Lakota elder chanted to the earth and the rising sun. We turned to the south, the west, the north, and the east in turn as the chant affirmed the virtues of each direction. During the chanting, I heard and saw the earth sigh and then felt and saw the earth breathing as she heaved rhythmically. Tears came to my eyes. The Sioux Nation has suffered and been so traumatized in these Black Hills, and Mother Earth was feeling their pain.

Seven virtues comprise the seven laws of the Lakota. They are to be practiced daily. Of course, it is cardinal that we treat other humans with the dignity of these seven virtues, but we should also extend them to the spirits of all creations—including insects, four-legged animals, and creatures that fly and swim—and to all manifestations of Mother Earth, including plants, rocks, rivers, mountains, and fire.

I joined the group of fire guardians who kept the sacred fire going through the long hours of the night. Fire is a shape-shifter and has the potential to rage out of control. But it was clear that the spirit of fire comes from Mother Earth. Everything, without exception, comes from Mother Earth: the food we eat, the water we drink, the air we breathe. Automobiles, computers, designer clothes, roof tiles, electricity, and granite countertops all come from Mother Earth. When we do not adequately respect and honor her and have compassion for all her creations, we lose our connection and begin to exploit her. With the climate crisis and the poisoning of our water and air, we can all see the consequences that occur when we forget that we are part of Mother Earth and that she is part of us.

Everyone wants to leave the ever-flowing stream. When you experience your connectedness with everyone and everything and your own self, you are no longer in the stream.

Each is still sitting in darkness black as charcoal.

Dr. Kent Brantley, who treated Ebola patients in Liberia and is an Ebola survivor himself, said, "Losing so many patients, certainly, was difficult, but it didn't make me feel like a failure as a physician because I had learned that there was so much more to being a physician than curing illness. That's not the most important thing we do. The most important thing we do is enter into the suffering of others."[8]

I take his statement to be indicative of the attitude of the fifth rank. It means to be exactly where you are, working with precisely what's in front of you, to enter completely into everything as it is. When I am sad, I am sad. When I am happy, I am happy.

Shunryu Suzuki wrote, "The Lotus Sutra says, to light up one corner of the world—that is enough. Not the whole world. Just make it clear where you are."[9]

Aitken Roshi translated this last line of Tozan's verse for the fifth rank as: "Not just to live in harmony, but to return and sit by the charcoal fire." Don't be fooled. You might think that the bodhisattva is warming herself by the fire in a state of repose. The fire is warm and comfortable, but it is not static. Just like Tokuun, who carries the mystic peak of Myobucho with him wherever he goes, the bodhisattva carries the cozy fire with her wherever she goes.

Chosha (Ch. Changsha Jingcen) went roaming the mountains one day. On returning, when he came to the gate, the head monk said, "Where have you been, Master?"

Chosha said, "Roaming the mountains."

The head monk said, "Where did you go?"

Chosha said, "First I followed the fragrant grasses on the way out. Then I came back pursuing the falling flowers."

The head monk said, "How very much like the sense of spring."

Chosha said, "It even surpasses the autumn dew dripping on the lotuses." (*Blue Cliff Record*, case 36)

The head monk is stiff and stern in questioning the master about why the latter is not taking care of the other monks and the monastery. Chosha is freely following the fragrant grasses and the falling flowers. Then he tells the head monk that it is better to be warm and receptive like the spring than to be cool and aloof like the autumn.

It is better to sit by the warm fire, covered with the ashes from all the turmoil and chaos of life, than to close the door and keep the drafts and riffraff out. Take the mystic peak of Myobucho with you wherever you go.

"People often ask me what is the most effective technique for transforming their life," wrote Aldous Huxley. "It is a little embarrassing that after years and years of research and experimentation, I have to say that the best answer is—just be a little kinder."[10]

Likewise, when asked about the nature of his Buddhist religion, the Dalai Lama often replied, "My religion is kindness."

Kindness is without limit. Our practice is endless. When waters of the ever-flowing stream finally reach the sea, they become the great waves that spread the Buddha's teachings in all ten directions.

To practice endlessly, to sit open-heartedly in darkness black as charcoal—that requires patience. Indeed, due to the various kinds of suffering and their causes, this life is sometimes referred to as the "land of patience." Without being patient, we cannot survive. One of the names of the Buddha is He Who Is Able to Be Patient. The Buddha said that being patient is far better than maintaining the precepts or practicing asceticism. Sometimes when we sit, we get impatient. If you are really patient, you don't get frustrated.

I once read the following presentation of *kshanti paramita*, which is the "perfection of patience," or simply the capacity to be with what is. A *paramita* is an aspect of the bodhisattva that can take us from the shore of suffering to the shore of enlightenment. Thus, the patience paramita takes us to the other shore through the agency of patience.

The essence of this paramita of patience is the strength of mind and heart that enables us to face the challenges and difficulties of life without losing our composure and inner tranquility. We embrace and forbear adversity, insult, distress, and the wrongs of others with patience and tolerance, free of resentment, irritation, emotional reactivity, or retaliation. We cultivate the ability to be loving and compassionate in the face of criticism, misunderstanding, or

aggression. With this enlightened quality of patience,
we are neither elated by praise, prosperity, or agree-
able circumstances, nor are we angry, unhappy
or depressed when faced with insult, challenge,
hardship, or poverty. This enlightened attribute of
patience, acceptance, and tolerance is not a forced
suppression or denial of our thoughts and feelings.
Rather, it is a quality of being which comes from
having our heart open and our mind deeply concentrated upon the Dharma. In this way, we have a
clear and correct understanding of impermanence, of
cause and effect (or karma), and with strong determination and patience we remain in harmony with
this understanding for the benefit of all beings. The
ability to endure, to have forbearance, is integral to
our Dharma practice. Without this kind of patience
we cannot accomplish anything.[11]

Of course, such perfection of patience is difficult to achieve.
One way to approach it is taking one step at a time. There is
a Spanish aphorism that goes like this: *Poco a poco, se va lejos*
("Little by little, one goes a long way"). Pay attention to those
small things that irritate you. Breathe into your irritation
and find your still point in the midst of upset. Do that to
each irritation as it arises, and little by little, your deportment will become attuned with the land of patience.

When we have attained unity and arrive in the midst
of relative/absolute, we have embodied all of the previous
ranks and intuitively know how to act in accord with our

new vision. We are beyond dualities, have left the ever-flowing stream, and know how to sit in the darkness black as charcoal. Yet the path does not end here. We have to keep infusing our attention and our intention into our practice.

One way to capture this ongoingness of the path is Dogen's teaching of *continuous practice*, meaning that one is mindful 24/7. Your attention is on call at all hours, even when reading on the toilet. Awakened mind calls to awakened mind 24/7. The ten thousand dharmas call to the awakened mind. The awakened mind turns the ten thousand dharmas while simultaneously being turned by the ten thousand dharmas.

Enlightenment is the reality of life, without judgment, without concepts, without projections. Enlightenment does not mean that you understand everything and that you no longer have to practice. Even the Buddha practiced for many lifetimes. Realizing life's Great Matter, gaining the Way, or attaining satori only means that you have clarified the true meaning of practice, clearly understand in which direction you should proceed, and know where you should place your intention and value in your life. It provides you with a clear direction. There is no more speculation or equivocation. You are comfortable in not-knowing.

Not-knowing is most intimate. If we can be truly comfortable in the state of not-knowing, we are open to each moment as it arises. When our hearts are open in all situations, that is true intimacy.

My teacher, Maezumi Roshi, gave advice on how to continue boundless practice using these four precautions:

1. Avoid an intellectual understanding of Zen.
2. Avoid dwelling on emptiness.
3. Avoid the expectation of enlightenment.
4. Do not deny the experience of enlightenment.

Maezumi Roshi's fourth and last precaution is warning us about Buji Zen. Buji Zen is the rejection of the enlightenment experience, since we are all intrinsically enlightened. My Dharma grandfather, Yasutani Roshi, emphasized two aspects of practice and realization: the intrinsic and the experiential. The intrinsic fact that we have an enlightened nature is meaningless unless we experience it for ourselves. In his koan system, we often have to present a koan both from the intrinsic perspective and from the experiential perspective.

Dwelling nowhere, raise the bodhi mind, the Mind that seeks enlightenment for the sake of all beings. Seeking nothing, raise the bodhi mind. How do we do that? We can be aware of Maezumi Roshi's four precautions in our practice: not clinging to intellectual understanding, not clinging to emptiness, not expecting enlightenment, and not rejecting enlightenment. So, how do we do it? As Master Yakusan said, "Even the Saints don't know." (*Transmission of Light*, Thirty-Sixth Ancestor). Just empty ourselves more and more and more, and don't cling. And from our zazen, everything else will spring forth.

o   o   o   o   o

PRACTICE QUESTION

How do you go beyond what is and what is not?

How do you understand "leaving the ever-flowing stream" and "sitting in darkness black as charcoal"?

8

New Perspectives on the Hensho Goi

IN THIS CHAPTER, we review the Hensho Goi and look at them, as a collective, through different lenses. (See also appendices A, B, and C for more views on the Hensho Goi.) Here again are my translations of all five:

1. The relative in the midst of the absolute
2. The absolute in the midst of the relative
3. Coming in the midst of the absolute
4. Reaching in the midst of the relative
5. Arriving in the midst of absolute/relative (unity realized)

Each facet of this spiritual jewel that has been cut so laboriously and painstakingly has to be polished to illuminate, correlate, and enhance your understanding. In the next section, we will appreciate how Dogen's writing shed new light on the Hensho Goi. Although Dogen lived four hundred years after Tozan and grew up in a different country, his writings can be used to clarify and deepen our understanding of the Five Ranks.

DOGEN'S "GENJOKOAN" AND THE HENSHO GOI

The most famous lines of Dogen's *Shobogenzo*, "Genjokoan" ("The Way of Everyday Life"), correspond directly to the Hensho Goi, and examining them can give us help toward a deeper understanding of each rank.

Dogen's verse is as follows:

> To study the Buddha Way is to study the self.
> To study the self is to forget the self.
> To forget the self is to be enlightened by the ten
>   thousand dharmas.
> To be enlightened by the ten thousand dharmas is to
>   free one's body and mind and those of others.
> No trace of enlightenment remains.
> And this traceless enlightenment is continued forever.

I have created a chart including the Five Ranks, these phrases from "Genjokoan," and the Zen Peacemaker interpretations of the Hensho Goi by Bernie Glassman. I have included the latter because in the course of presenting the Five Ranks in different venues, I have gotten feedback from participants that Bernie Glassman's interpretation made conceptual sense to them and allowed them to penetrate into the traditional translations.

TRADITIONAL FIVE RANKS	PEACEMAKER	GENJOKOAN
		To study the Buddha Way is to study the self.
1. The relative in the midst of the absolute	Absolute bearing witness to the relative	To study the self is to forget the self.
2. The absolute in the midst of the relative	Relative bearing witness to the absolute	To forget the self is to be enlightened by the 10,000 dharmas.
3. Coming in the midst of the absolute	Bearing witness to the absolute	To be enlightened by the 10,000 dharmas is to free one's body and mind and those of others.
4. Reaching in the midst of the relative	Bearing witness to the relative	No trace of enlightenment remains.
5. Arriving in the midst of absolute/ relative	Bearing witness to life itself	And this traceless enlightenment is continued forever.

To Study the Self

The first line of Dogen's verse is "To study the Buddha Way is to study the self." So, when we start on the path of our practice, that's what we are doing. The first instruction in zazen is to quiet the mind. You need to focus your mind on something that's rhythmic and steady, like your breathing, to connect with the self that exists beneath all the chatter of your mind. This is the start of the journey.

To Forget the Self

At the beginning of our practice, we notice that all of our mental activity is generally designed to protect our ego identification from any kind of intrusion so that it feels safe. The ego self just wants whatever is comfortable, whatever feels safe, whatever maintains it. Drawing on its survival mechanisms, the ego simply tries to push away the whole notion of impermanence. But as you sit more and more, you notice how thoughts arise, persist, and then decay. Then you start to see these little gaps between the thoughts. Your image of who you are starts to dissolve, and you begin to realize that "to study the self is to forget the self."

This line of Dogen's corresponds to the first of the Five Ranks, "the relative in the midst of the absolute," with its verse line "no wonder they meet without knowing each other." In the first rank, the practitioner experiences the emptiness of self and no longer knows who they are. It is the absolute state wherein there is nothing to grasp. The absolute is bearing witness to the relative, since the practitioner embodies the absolute state while functioning in the relative state. And the relative is in the midst of the absolute.

This first rank and Dogen's line "to forget the self" are illustrated in the famous koan, case 41 of *The Gateless Gate*, which records a dialogue between Bodhidharma and his successor Master Eka (Ch. Dazu Huike).

Eka went to Bodhidharma and said, "My mind is not at peace, please pacify it for me."

Bodhidharma replied, "Bring me your mind and I will pacify it for you."

Eka said, "I have exhaustively searched for this mind, and it is ungraspable."

Bodhidharma responded, "Then I have pacified it for you."

The key phrase in this koan is "I have exhaustively searched for this mind, and it is ungraspable." Within that phrase there are two key words. One is *exhaustively*. That's what Zen masters tell us over and over. If you are working on a koan, exhaust it. Exhaust the mind. The beginning of Dogen's *Shobogenzo*, "Bendowa" ("The Wholehearted Way"), contains the line, "After searching exhaustively, the way is perfect and all-pervading." It is only "after searching exhaustively" that you realize the perfect and all-pervading nature of the Way.

Eka says, "After searching exhaustively, I find that mind is ungraspable"—and that is the second key word: *ungraspable*. He is not saying, "I cannot grasp it." He is saying that the very nature of mind is that it is ungraspable.

To exhaustively study the self is to forget the self. You have to penetrate every nook and cranny looking for it and let go of everything you think is it. It's not that. It's not that. It's not that. Then you get down to the fine dust and start running it through your fingers and looking for the self. Is it that? Search forever, and you will not find the self. When you realize that the self is ungraspable, you have realized the "to forget the self" of which Dogen speaks and the "meet without knowing each other" of which Tozan speaks.

To Be Enlightened by the Ten Thousand Dharmas

Dogen goes on to say, "To forget the self is to be enlightened by the ten thousand dharmas." What are the ten thousand dharmas? The dharmas are the phenomenal world, and in the classical Sino-Japanese context, "ten thousand dharmas" means everything. The verse for the second rank, "the absolute in the midst of the relative," says, "She finds her ancient mirror and she clearly sees her face which cannot be elsewhere." Her true face is everywhere. It is no longer obscured by the false egoic self. It is the ten thousand dharmas. It is the relative bearing witness to the absolute. Because the practitioner has experienced the absolute, they are able to see it everywhere they look.

A teacher once told me that I should hear every sound as the Dharma. He said *dharma* has multiple meanings, and in this case, the Dharma is the teachings of the Buddha. So, hear every sound as the teachings of the Buddha. Be enlightened by the ten thousand sounds.

If you read the stories of the Zen masters, there were all kinds of occasions where they became enlightened by one of the ten thousand dharmas, such as Zen Master Kyogen becoming awakened to the sound of a pebble hitting bamboo. Another Zen master became enlightened while he was going to the bathroom. One monk was awakened when his leg was crushed in a door. To forget the self is to be enlightened by the ten thousand dharmas, and any dharma might do the trick. Hear every sound as the sound of the Dharma. See every sight as the sight of the Dharma. Experience every place as nirvana. This very cushion upon which you sit is the lotus land. The old woman's ancient mirror reflects her face, which is none other than the ten thousand dharmas.

To Free One's Body and Mind and Those of Others

Dogen's verse continues: "To be enlightened by the ten thousand dharmas is to free one's body and mind and those of others." The verse of Tozan's third rank, "coming in the midst of the absolute," states that "in the midst of nothing, there is a way free from dust." So, one must free one's body and mind. But how?

This relates to the koan that Dogen Zenji was working on when he had his enlightenment experience. According to the account in *Transmission of Light*, the Fifty-First Ancestor, Dogen and the other monks were sitting when his teacher said, "Drop off body and mind." Let your mind and body fall away. Liberate your body and mind.

How do you free your body and mind and those of others? Bernie Glassman said, "Bear witness to the absolute." In the act of bearing witness to the absolute, you realize that you and all beings everywhere are intimately connected. There is no separation between "me" and all beings everywhere. When you free your body and mind, you simultaneously free those of others. That's what the Buddha said when he became enlightened: "I and all beings everywhere have simultaneously attained enlightenment." (*Transmission of Light*, case I)

No Trace of Enlightenment Remains

The last line of Dogen's verse starts, "No trace of enlightenment remains." No trace remains. This is where the contradictions of life end. The seventh of the ten ox-herding pictures shows the enlightened person resting in his hut and no trace of the ox exists. This corresponds to Tozan's fourth rank, "reaching in the midst of the relative," the verse for which says, "There is no need to avoid crossed swords." Bearing witness to the relative is "a good hand, like a lotus blooming in a fire." Tozan's verse for this rank and Dogen's line teach us how to live in the relative without being trapped by the relative. Being selfless, one can act according to conditions without hanging on to anything.

This Traceless Enlightenment Continues Forever

According to Tozan's verse for the fifth rank, "arriving in the midst of absolute/relative," we are all "sitting in the darkness as black as charcoal." What a beautiful image for ongoing traceless enlightenment. There is light within the darkness, and we could just as easily say that we are sitting in the light as clear as the bright sky. These metaphors represent the bodhisattva's practice, which is endless. It is not just sitting. It also includes standing, walking, and dancing. Our bodhisattva activity and the effects of this traceless enlightenment continue forever. When we fully engage in our lives, when we "bear witness to life itself"—in the words of the Zen Peacemaker version of this rank—there is no end and no beginning to life. Generation after generation, this traceless enlightenment continues.

If you are not careful, you can get stuck anywhere. When you practice meticulously, no trace of enlightenment remains, whatever you realize and whatever you reveal.

As mentioned in chapter 5, a Chinese proverb says, "Having nothing is better than having something good." That's why this enlightenment is traceless and continues forever. So, how does it feel? As one teacher said, "There is no firm ground upon which to stand." Isn't that marvelous? Isn't that liberating? No firm ground upon which to stand. This is one of the dharma seals of the Buddha: impermanence. The three dharma seals of the Buddha are impermanence, no-self, and nirvana. They describe this very place, this very moment, this very second.

These lines from the "Genjokoan" and the Hensho Goi tell us very clearly how our practice is to proceed.

KYUHO'S HEAD AND TAIL

Another useful example to clarify the Hensho Goi is case 66 from *The Book of Equanimity*, "Kyuho's Head and Tail." This koan corresponds to the Hensho Goi, with the head representing the absolute, or enlightenment, and the tail the relative, or practice. We can also see the head as wisdom and the tail as compassion.

Attention! A monk asked Kyuho, "What is the head?"

Kyuho said, "Opening the eyes and not being aware of the dawn."

The monk asked, "What is the tail?"

Kyuho said, "Not sitting on an eternal seat."

The monk asked, "What about having the head and no tail?"

Kyuho said, "After all, it's not precious."

The monk asked, "What about having the tail and no head?"

Kyuho said, "Though satisfied, you are powerless."

The monk asked, "How about when head and tail are directly well matched."

Kyuho replied, "A descendant gains power without knowing it."

See the following chart for how this koan's lines parallel the Hensho Goi.

HENSHO GOI	KYUHO'S HEAD AND TAIL
1. The relative in the midst of the absolute	A monk asked Kyuho, "What is the head?" Kyuho said, "Opening the eyes and not being aware of the dawn."
2. The absolute in the midst of the relative	The monk asked, "What is the tail?" Kyuho said, "Not sitting on an eternal seat."
3. Coming in the midst of the absolute	The monk asked, "What about having the head and no tail?" Kyuho said, "After all, it's not precious."
4. Reaching in the midst of the relative	The monk asked, "What about having the tail and no head?" Kyuho said, "Though satisfied, you are powerless."
5. Arriving in the midst of absolute/relative	The monk asked, "How about when head and tail are directly well matched?" Kyuho replied, "A descendant gains power without knowing it."

What is the head?

Answering this question, Kyuho said, "Opening the eyes and not being aware of the dawn." This sounds like Tozan's verse for the first Hensho Goi:

> Early in the evening before the moon shines
> No wonder they meet without knowing each other.

There is no self and no other and no recognition or awareness. That is the state of the relative in the midst of the absolute.

At a different time, Kyuho's teacher, Sekiso, was asked these same questions by his community. His responses are different, yet they also correspond to the Hensho Goi.[1]

Sekiso started by saying, "Beginners who have not yet gotten the Great Matter, who have not yet penetrated into their essential nature, first should know that the head and tail should come of themselves."

When asked, "What's the head?" Sekiso replied, "You should know that it exists." There is such a thing as enlightenment. Don't deny it. Our essential nature is the same as that of buddhas, but without practice, we don't realize it.

What is the tail?

Kyuho's response to this question means "Will you keep sitting on the eternal seat of the absolute, satisfying yourself but unable to help others?" He implores his monks to get down from the eternal seat and engage in the world of chaos, confusion, and suffering. That's the value of this second rank, "the absolute in the midst of the relative." As Tozan versified, "No more will you reject your head by grasping at its shadow."

To "What's the tail?" Sekiso responded, "Exhausting the present." That's what our practice is—exhausting the present. Penetrate through every thought, every feeling, every sensation, every conception, every perception. Just be aware of it. Don't stop and identify yourself as a particular thought or perception. Totally exhaust every corner. If you're holding on to anything, any image of who you think you should be, you're not exhausting it. You have to be willing to totally expose yourself, whatever it is that you're hiding. You will see your face in the ancient mirror, which cannot be elsewhere. Everywhere you look, whether at the sky, across a lake, or in the eyes of your beloved, you see your own reflection. In this rank, you bear witness to your connection with the universe.

What about having the head and no tail?

As Kyuho said, "After all, it's not precious." Everything Midas touched turned to gold. Sounds good in the abstract. But then he touched his daughter, and she became a gold statue. What a horror! If you shine brightly, what's the purpose? To blind other people? Tozan versified about this third rank, "coming in the midst of the absolute": "Hard though it may be in the midst of nothing, there is a way free from dust." The way free from dust is to not cherish the absolute or "nothing." Sekiso said, "What's the use of spitting out gold?"

What about having the tail and no head?

If there's a tail and no head, Kyuho said, "Though satisfied, you are powerless." In terms of wisdom and compassion, in this state, one would have lots of compassion but inadequate wisdom to put it into practice in an appropriate way. Such a person would run around trying to do good but might make more of a mess. Sometimes this is called idiot compassion. As an example, the use of DDT to control mosquitos that carry malaria caused disruption in the ecosystem and introduced the poison into fish and ultimately predators, including humans. Ignorance is bliss. You are satisfied, but you don't have the wisdom to be effective.

In response to this question, Sekiso said, "There's still dependence." You haven't quite let go. There's still something there. Although your deportment might be exemplary, your vision is still clouded, and your insight is not thorough. Tozan said, "A good hand, like a lotus blooming in a fire / has in itself a heaven-soaring spirit." There is still attachment there. You are dependent on conditions and are buffeted about on the winds of change, rather than sailing on the winds.

How about when head and tail are directly well matched?

What about when the head and tail are well matched? Kyuho said, "The descendent becomes powerful without knowing it." The descendent is Kyuho's successor, who has realized the subtle significance of the fifth rank, "arriving in the midst of absolute/relative." Tozan's verse says that though they want to leave the ever-flowing stream, each is still sitting in darkness black as charcoal. Without thinking about it and without expecting accolades, they do their bodhisattva work endlessly.

On this point, Sekiso said, "Even if he does understand this, I don't yet approve of him!" If the practitioner understands this, there's still something left to understand. When Tozan asked, "Who can be tuned to that beyond what is and what is not?" he challenged us to go beyond conceptual understanding and become intimate with not-knowing.

What this koan and these teachers are telling us is that first we practice and raise our intention. We raise our determination to practice and have some realization. Then let go of that and continue to practice. That's what Zen is; there's no beginning and no end. Just practice-realization. Letting go. Further practice. If we see it clearly, we will know that this division into head and tail is artificial. It is really bogus. It's just an expedient means to help you understand what you're going through with practice and to further clarify it.

Kyuho said, "When ancients spoke of the head, it was only to let you know that it exists. Speaking of the tail was just to make you use the present time to its fullest. If someone is essentially so, real and true, always thus, then they shouldn't talk about this anymore." After all, if the absolute is truly absolute, how could it exist anywhere other than here? There's no other place for it to be. There's no other place for us to be.

No head and no tail. They're not two sides. It's your life. Just let it be so. Just reveal who you truly are and manifest that as your life. It's worth repeating what Maezumi Roshi often used to say: "Appreciate your life."

THE FIVE RANKS OF THE SEQUENCE OF MERIT

IN ADDITION TO the more well-known Hensho Goi, Master Tozan articulated a second set of Five Ranks called Kokun Goi, which, roughly translated, means "Sequence of Merit Five Ranks." They are:

1. Shift
2. Submission
3. Achievement or awakening
4. Collective achievement or collective awakening
5. Absolute achievement or absolute awakening

The Hensho Goi, the Five Ranks of the relative and absolute, are said to contain each other. Maezumi Roshi used the analogy of a balloon, in that every point on the balloon supports the whole structure. When we talk about the absolute in the first rank, it can only be understood in terms of the relative.

So, the first two ranks are dependent on each other. The third and fourth ranks are independent in that the third emphasizes the absolute, and the fourth emphasizes the relative. Yet neither could exist without the other. The fifth Hensho rank comprises all the other four together. But none of them could be accurately articulated if the others did not exist. You can picture the Hensho Goi as a circular path— or a spiral path might be more apt. You never end up at the same place you started.

The Five Ranks of the Kokun Goi are more linear, or ascending—containing a sense of pro-gression. In that sense, they are similar to the ten ox-herding pictures, which describe the progression of Zen practice. (See appendix D.) I should point out, however, that these stages in the Kokun Goi and the ox-herding pictures are not exact steps that each practitioner follows in their practice. They simply give an overall idea but can vary in each person's case. In some instances, the order of the stages may not be exact. Like so many descriptions and expla-nations in Zen, even these more linear descriptions are the finger pointing at the moon. They are not the moon.

As with the Hensho Goi, each of the Kokun Goi has a verse by Tozan. We will examine each line of the verse and treat them as koans, as we did in the earlier chapters. Furthermore, each of the Kokun Goi has a question from a monk asking about the rank and Tozan's answer. These exchanges appear in

The Record of Tozan and will be reproduced and commented on in each respective chapter.

There are fewer English translations of the Kokun Goi than there are of the Hensho Goi. I have included three different translations at the beginning of each chapter to allow you to see the nuances of each translator's interpretation. I will emphasize the translations that Maezumi Roshi used in our studies. They are primarily from Charles Luk's *Ch'an and Zen Teaching*.

Aitken Roshi wrote that the Kokun Goi are related to the Hensho Goi as the manner is to the substance of Zen practice.[1] In both *The Record of Tozan* and the teachings of Maezumi Roshi, the two series of Five Ranks are treated as being independent of each other. I will take that approach here.

9

First Kokun Goi

Shift

Following the example set by Emperor Yao
The prince teaches morality to his people.
At times he passes by the noisy market place,
While all men welcome his royal rule.

(Luk, Ch'an and Zen Teaching)

The sage kings from the beginning made Yao the
    norm;
He governed the people by means of rites and kept
    his dragon-waist bent
When once he passed from one end of the market
    to the other,
He found that everywhere culture flourished and
    the august dynasty was celebrated.

(Powell, The Record of Tung-shan)

As the sacred master, make the way of Yao your own:
He governed with propriety, and bent the dragon
    waist;
When he passed through a market, he found culture
    flourishing—
And the august dynasty celebrated everywhere.

                    (Aitken, *The Morning Star*)

I T SHOULD COME as no surprise that the Kokun Goi open with the idea of a shift—after all, impermanence is one of the central teachings of Buddhism. We have all kinds of shifts in our lives, and indeed, the shifts never stop! But the first Kokun Goi intends the word *shift* to be understood in a particular way—the shift from dwelling in samsara, or delusion, toward taking a path of awakening.

This first Kokun Goi aligns with the first of the ten ox-herding pictures, in which the ox represents our true nature. The first picture is titled "Searching for the Ox," and the commentary on this picture states:

"Why the search? The ox has never been missing from the beginning. However, when you turn away from yourself, your own ox becomes a stranger and eventually you get lost in the far, dusty regions. Desire for profit and fear of loss flare up like a raging fire and views of right and wrong arise in opposition to one another, like spears on a battlefield."[1]

From such a state of being, what can give rise to this shift?

People are attracted to Zen for a wide range of reasons, all of which are valid. It could be that you took a class on Buddhism and heard the teachings, enabling you to intellectually grasp something of the meaning of Truth. Maybe you met a spiritual friend who encouraged you to shift. Or you may have had a glimpse of emptiness, an experience beyond your usual perception of reality, and you wanted to understand what that was about.

This variety notwithstanding, newcomers to Zen do tend to have a few things in common. Underneath whatever intellectual curiosity or fleeting experience of emptiness may be there, they are not satisfied with their lives as they are, or they have big questions about the meaning of life. That dissatisfaction could range from mild discomfort to dis-ease to severe anxiety and depression. In some cases, they are faced with the realities of sickness, old age, and death, just like the Buddha during his sojourn from the palace.

There is a recognition that you have to change your life or there will be no peace, tranquility, or equanimity. The path of meditation now appears as a real possibility for you.

First you put one toe on the path and then a whole foot. You encounter others who have decided to follow the path of meditation, and they encourage you to continue, and you see something compelling about them that urges you on. Have you made a commitment, or is it just another fad that has caught your fancy? The shift has to be present and effective from top to bottom.

You have to jump in and learn to swim, or your inner light will keep shining somewhere other than at the source of your discontent. Where do you suppose that would be?

Don't be like the drunk who was looking for his keys at night under a lamp post. A passerby offered to help and asked the drunk where he lost his keys. He pointed out into the dark and said, "Over there, somewhere."

The passerby said, "Why are you looking here?"

The drunk answered, "There's no light over there."

Shine your light where your key resides, which is always in your own heart. To study Zen is to study the self.

In my own life, the stage of shift was not solely a matter of starting to meditate. It permeated every aspect of my life. I quit spending time with old friends who just wanted to party and obliterate themselves, preferring to spend my time with friends who wanted to obliterate themselves through meditation. I did not use my vacation time to luxuriate on the beach of a tropical isle but for years used all of it to attend *sesshin*. Can you imagine? Although recreational drugs played a role in bringing me to Zen, once I realized that they were no longer going to help, I cut back and then quit using them. If the shift does not occur off the cushion as well as on the cushion, it is only a partial shift. Each of us has to follow our own heart and go at our own pace. Once I saw the value of Zen in my life and in the lives of others, I did not hold back.

One of the most famous stories of a significant shift is *A Christmas Carol* by Charles Dickens. The protagonist, Ebenezer Scrooge, is a mean-spirited, tight-fisted miser and skeptic. He is visited by a ghost and three spirits who point out his stingy ways and severely scare him into changing his behavior. The ghost of his old partner, Jacob Marley, tells him that he will suffer eternally if he keeps on the path he is on. The end of the story reveals a radically transformed Scrooge who makes anonymous gifts to charity, honors the Christmas season, and raises the salary of his employee, Bob Cratchit. Finally, he becomes a grandfather figure to Tiny Tim. What causes him to shift? Besides being frightened by the consequences of his behavior, I think it is the unhappiness of being lonely and without any warm human connections.

Perhaps the shift that brought you to Zen practice had some of the same elements. A loss of intimacy is a very common reason that people come to Zen. As we have already discussed, vulnerability is a precursor to intimacy, and not-knowing is the most intimate. It is about being open, particularly open to change, which is the nature of this first Kokun Goi.

A monk asked Master Tozan, "What is the meaning of *shift*?"

Tozan replied, "What do you do when eating rice?"

When you are eating your rice, do you just eat your rice, or are you drifting off to all kinds of thoughts about the external world while absentmindedly eating your rice?

An old Zen story tells of a student who said to Master Ichu, "Please write for me something of great wisdom."

Master Ichu picked up his brush and wrote one word: "Attention."

The student said, "Is that all?"

The master wrote, "Attention. Attention."

The student became irritable. "That doesn't seem profound or subtle to me."

In response, Master Ichu wrote simply, "Attention. Attention. Attention."

In frustration, the student demanded, "What does this word 'attention' mean?"

Master Ichu replied, "Attention means attention."[2]

Even if we have felt a yearning to shift or even experienced the beginning of shifting, how easy it is for our attention to fade. We usually focus on how we want things to be different than they are. If we were content, we would not be constantly searching outside ourselves for happiness and satisfaction.

How can we turn the light around and fix our attention toward the process of the shift? During jukai, the ceremony of receiving the Buddhist precepts, we vow to maintain those precepts. At the most fundamental level, it means that you reveal your life as those precepts. Through continual meditation practice, these vows emerge from your heart. They are not imposed from an outside authority. It is not a question of following some moral teaching; you are the moral teaching itself. Maintaining these vows, which continue without end, is a shift.

Now let's look at Tozan's verse for the first Kokun Goi:

Following the example set by Emperor Yao
The emperor teaches the way to live to his people
    generously.
At times he passes by the noisy market place,
While all men welcome his royal rule.

Let's consider each line.

Following the example set by Emperor Yao

Emperor Yao, said to have reigned for one hundred years from 2357–2257 B.C.E., is one of the celebrated rulers of ancient China. In this verse, he represents the Buddha and our Zen ancestors, and I read the line straightforwardly as an encouragement to follow the example of a role model.

We all need role models to see what is possible. As a young Jewish boy, I loved sports, but there were not a lot of famous Jewish athletes to emulate. There were a number of great Jewish boxers, such as Maxie Baer and Benny Leonard, but I did not love boxing, I loved baseball. Hall of Fame baseball player Hank Greenberg was Jewish, but he played for the Detroit Tigers, not one of my favorite teams. Sandy Koufax almost fit the bill, but he came along too late. Even though he played for my favorite team, the Los Angeles Dodgers, he was a pitcher, and I preferred other positions.

I could never find the "Emperor Yao" Jewish baseball player I was looking for, so I looked elsewhere and found inspiration in reading about Albert Einstein. He was brilliant, compassionate, and Jewish. He might have had something to do with my choosing to study physics, but there was something else. I wanted to know all the mysteries of the universe. That quest finally led me to Buddhism. I try to follow the example of the Buddha, of my teachers (at least the best part of my teachers), my parents (also, their best parts), and my other mentors in academia and business.

Years ago, I was fortunate to attend a conference that had Elisabeth Kübler-Ross as a speaker, and she became an inspiration to me. She was a Swiss-American psychiatrist who pioneered the modern study of death and dying. There was a lot of resistance in the traditional medical community to her area of interest. In the hospital where she worked, the doctors avoided confronting the fact that patients were dying in their wards. The inevitability of death was like the elephant in the room.

Kübler-Ross persisted and eventually gained begrudging approval of her studies. She even received enough grant money to hire an assistant. She didn't hire a nurse or a medical assistant. She hired the black cleaning lady on her ward, who was comfortable with the patients who were dying. This woman had held her own child in her arms while the child died. She was no stranger to death. Their work helped initiate a big shift in the awareness of and attention to death and dying in the helping professions.

Dr. Kübler-Ross was a major proponent of the hospice and palliative care movement, founding a number of hospice programs herself. She was also known for formulating the five stages of grief model: denial, anger, bargaining, depression, and acceptance. Although this grief model has been superseded in recent years, she broke the ground for later approaches to grief counseling.[3]

Just as it is important to find and appreciate inspiring role models, it is important to realize that each of us is an example for others. If we are parents, we are examples for our children. If we are teachers, we are examples for our students. If we are entrepreneurs or business owners, we are examples for our employees.

There is a saying that when you become a Zen teacher, it is like putting on an iron yoke. Your life is an open book and an example for others. As Master Tozan said, "As to that, I always take heed." (*Book of Equanimity*, case 98)

The emperor teaches the way to live to his people generously.

What was it that caused you to shift? Did you read a book that a Zen master generously wrote to share the Dharma? Did you resonate with a sutra that you heard? Did a friend encourage you to meditate with them?

Recall the story of Huineng, the Sixth Ancestor in China, who heard a monk reciting the Diamond Sutra in the marketplace. The lines "Dwelling in no place, / raise the Bodhi mind" resonated so strongly with Huineng that he had a deep experience of awakening.

In 1965 I read *The Three Pillars of Zen*, edited by Philip Kapleau. It was the first book about actual Zen practice published in the United States. Previous books about Zen theory or with stories of Zen masters had been published, but they did not tell you how to meditate. I was struck by the book and especially by the chapter describing the enlightenment experiences of the Zen students. They inspired me to shift and begin to practice. I set out to study the way in all earnestness.

Reading *The Three Pillars of Zen* was both a blessing and a curse. It was a blessing for getting me on the path. The curse was that I became so smitten with one of the enlightenment experiences that I wanted to duplicate it for myself. It was the kensho experience of Koun Yamada, who later became a roshi and whom I fortunately met in Japan.

Yamada Roshi's experience came while he was reading the following phrase from a seventeenth-century Zen text: "I came to realize clearly that Mind is no other than mountains and rivers and the great wide earth, the sun, the moon and the stars." Suddenly the bottom dropped out of his fixed perceptions, and he deeply comprehended this statement. He cried and laughed uncontrollably and told his wife, "In my present exhilarated frame of mind I could rise to the greatest heights."[4]

I followed the meditation instructions in the book and tried for several years to emulate Yamada Roshi's experience, until I realized that I was not Yamada Roshi. I needed to shift further, shine the light within myself, and have my own experiences.

One of the most famous Zen stories about shift involves Master Tokusan, who lived in the north of China and was a wonderful scholar. He knew all the sutras and was particularly expert on the Diamond Sutra, earning the nickname King of the Diamond Sutra.

Tokusan had heard that in the south of China, Zen schools claimed that you can be suddenly enlightened in just one moment. According to Tokusan's understanding of the sutra, it didn't quite say that, so he felt he had better go south and set the record straight for all the monks and Zen masters down there. He collected his commentaries on the Diamond Sutra and started south.

As he was traveling, he came to a fork in the road where an old woman was selling tea. He wanted to buy a cake from her because he was hungry. She looked at him and said, "Tell me, what is that you are carrying?"

He replied, "Oh, I am the King of the Diamond Sutra. These are my commentaries, and I have come down here to the southern part of China so that I can clarify the essential teachings."

The woman said, "Oh, is that so? I have a question about the Diamond Sutra, and if you can answer it for me, I will give you the cake. If you can't answer it, I won't give you anything."

He said, "Go ahead and ask me, old woman."

So, she asked, "In the Diamond Sutra it says that the mind of the past is ungraspable, and the mind of the future is ungraspable, and the mind of the present is ungraspable. Then, with which mind are you going to eat this cake?"

Tokusan didn't know how to answer. In the end, all of his commentaries had done him no good. But he had enough presence of mind to realize that this wasn't an ordinary tea lady, and he had enough humility to ask, "Is there a Zen master around here I can study with?"

The tea lady told him that he could find Zen Master Ryutan (Ch. Longtan Chongxin) just down the road. Tokusan decided to go study with Ryutan. Case 28 in *The Gateless Gate* describes the encounter between Tokusan and Ryutan:

> One night, Tokusan persisted in asking Ryutan for instruction, and Ryutan finally said, "The night is late. Why don't you go to bed?"
>
> Tokusan made his bows, raised the door curtain, and left. Seeing how dark the night was, he turned back and said, "It's pitch black outside."
>
> Ryutan lit a lantern and handed it to Tokusan. Just as Tokusan reached for it, Ryutan blew it out. At that Tokusan came to sudden realization and made a deep bow.

Ryutan asked, "What did you realize?"

Tokusan replied, "From now on I will not doubt the words of an old master who is renowned everywhere under the sun."

Tokusan had his eye of wisdom opened and saw clearly—not just with his rational mind but with his whole body and mind together. After his awakening experience, he took all of his commentaries and books and set them on fire in front of the zendo. Then, according to the case, he said, "Even though one masters various profound philosophies, it is like placing a single strand of hair in the great sky. Even if one gains all the essential knowledge in the world, it is like throwing a drop of water into a deep ravine." Tokusan was thus essentially agreeing with the Buddha's teaching in *The Sutra of Forty-Two Sections*: "If you endeavor to embrace the way through much learning, the way will not be understood. If you observe the way with simplicity of heart, great indeed is the way."[5]

How generously the Buddha, Ryutan, and Tokusan teach us to live the way.

At times he passes by the noisy market place,

In the noisy market, you don't see everything going on because it is chaotic, like your life. Whatever you do, whatever you say, whatever you think, regardless of the noise and chaos, that is the path—if you see it clearly. Then there is harmony everywhere.

Whatever happens, morning to night, keep practicing.

An exemplar for practicing with this kind of dedication, and bringing your practice to the noisy marketplace, is Jizo Bodhisattva (Skt. Kshitigarbha). Jizo is highly venerated in China and Japan as the protector of children and travelers, and as a guide to the afterlife. He made strong vows to remain in the world and save beings in all realms, especially the hell realms, until Maitreya Buddha, the future Buddha, appears.

Jizo's name means "Earth Storehouse" or "Earth Womb." He is strongly associated with the earth, and although he is depicted as a male monk in the Japanese tradition, we can consider him Mother Earth, as he expresses many aspects of mothering, protection, and nurturing.

In the Earth Store Sutra, Jizo says to the Buddha, "If good men and women of the future have even a single thought of respect for the Buddha's teachings, I shall use hundreds of thousands of expedient devices to lead them out of the suffering of Constant Birth and Death to liberation."[6]

That is the power of a vow. It is the life blood of our practice, and that is why at Great Mountain Zen Center we ask members to state their intentions for sesshin and for their practice. When despair descends, the power of your vows will bring direction and light to your practice and your life.

Jizo is a savior and guide for those in the underworld, or the hell realms, although he does his work in all realms. It is believed that of all the realms of existence described in Buddhist scriptures, the human realm is the most auspicious. This is because even though humans are beset with greed, hate, and ignorance, they do not suffer as much as those in the lower realms or become as enamored with pleasure as those in the higher realms, and thus have the capacity to raise the mind that seeks enlightenment. Due to the efforts of Jizo, however, it is also possible for those in the other realms of existence to pursue a spiritual path. His benevolence can transform hell dwellers into spiritual seekers and can help hungry ghosts to find a path to salvation. He even assists devas or those in the heavenly realms to forsake their blissful state and join those who have raised the bodhi mind, the mind that seeks enlightenment for the sake of everyone.

Jizo Bodhisattva is called the King of Vows. When we call upon him, we call upon our deepest vows, our deepest intentions, and our spiritually wholesome desires. We are calling upon the innate power within us that longs to fulfill our vow to realize our place and our purpose on this earth and to live lives that manifest this understanding, no matter how often we find ourselves passing by the noisy marketplace.

Once, a student went to Master Gensha and asked how he could enter Zen. Gensha asked if he heard the sound of the mountain stream.

The student said, "Yes, I do."

Then Gensha said to enter Zen from there.[7]

Do you hear the cackling of the black birds? Enter Zen from there. Do you smell the rain on the parched earth? Enter Zen from there. Do you hear the sound of traffic? Enter Zen from there. Did your partner or housemate complain that you left a mess in the kitchen? Enter Zen from there. Did you get discouraged reading the latest news about the environment or politics? Enter Zen from there.

Torei Zenji, a successor of Hakuin, wrote a wonderful verse called "Bodhisattva's Vow." It starts out like this: "When I (a student of the Dharma) look at the real form of the universe, all is the never-failing manifestation of the mysterious truth of Tathagata. In any event, in any moment, and in any place, none can be other than the marvelous revelation of its glorious light."[8]

How can he say that? In any event. In any moment. In any place. Torei Zenji does not leave any stone unturned. I am sure you can think of exceptions that certainly don't seem to be the marvelous revelation of the Tathagata's glorious light. But Torei Zenji makes no exceptions. Even the noisy, chaotic marketplace, which represents every moment of every job you've ever had. It includes every interaction with everybody in your life—even your sworn enemies. It includes every distasteful thing you have had to do, including cleaning the latrine or putting down a pet. Zen is everywhere.

As a Zen verse says, "On whose doorstep does the Sun not shine."

While all men welcome his royal rule.

The Identity of Relative and Absolute contains the line: "The four elements return to their nature as a child to its mother." Perhaps that line better captures the spirit of this final line of the first Kokun Goi verse for our age, given the patriarchal overtones of "men welcome his royal rule." That spirit is also nicely encapsulated in the following teaching from Dogen:

Roshin is the mind or attitude of a parent. In the
same way that a parent cares for an only child, keep
the Three Treasures in your heart. A parent, irrespec-
tive of poverty or difficult circumstances, loves and
raises a child with care. How deep is love like this?
Only a parent can understand it. A parent protects
the children from the cold and shades them from
the hot sun with no concern for his or her own personal welfare. Only a person in whom this mind has
arisen can understand it, and only one in whom this
attitude has become second nature can fully realize
it. This is the ultimate in being a parent. In this same
manner, when handling any affairs in your life, you
must have the affectionate and caring concern of a
parent raising a child. (*Shobogenzo*, "Tenzokyokun")

What happens when you welcome the royal rule of the
Dharma in your own life? It does not mean that you will
become the prime minister with lots of power. Quite the
contrary, you become the servant. In case 45 in *The Gateless
Gate*, it says, "Shakyamuni Buddha and Maitreya are servants
of another. Who is that other?"

Rabindranath Tagore, the Indian Nobel Prize–winning
writer, mystic, and philosopher, said, "I slept and dreamt
that life was joy. I awoke and saw that life was service. I
acted and behold, service was joy."[9]

"His dynasty is celebrated" is another translation of this
line. Several Zen centers have adapted the Twelve Steps of

Alcoholics Anonymous (AA) and made them relevant to those who follow the Buddhist faith. This line sounds like the second of the original Twelve Steps. In the Buddhist version, it is "We came to believe that a Power other than self could restore us to sanity."

You will be peaceful if you are in harmony with this second step of AA—or if you at least have faith in this path. In my case, I was willing to test or examine the path. I felt at home because I did not have to believe anything. I could find out for myself. So, I tried it. At first, it was like when I played golf. I took up golf to do something with my father. I was never good at it, but I would have about one par per eighteen holes. That was enough for me to return. I would go to sesshin, and physically it was very painful, but if I had one instant of clarity, it was enough for me to return.

Although in this first Kokun Goi you have found the path, you still cannot distinguish between what is genuine and what is not. The way keeps evolving. The reasons we started to practice are not the reasons we continue to practice. And our ideas and understanding about practice continue to evolve.

Your mind might not know for sure what is genuine, but your body does. Listen to your heart. Your heart knows when a shift is necessary. Once we shift, we need to continue shifting, for there is no safe, secure, and final ground upon which to stand.

o   o   o   o   o

PRACTICE QUESTION

Do you know what caused the experience of shift that led you to start following the path of the Buddha? What did you see or glimpse?

10

Second Kokun Goi

Submission

For whom is the elaborate toilette now discarded?
The cuckoo's call urges the traveler to turn home.
Its note continues when myriads of flowers have
     fallen,
Calling further, deep into the intermingling peaks.

(Luk, Ch'an and Zen Teaching)

For whom do you wash your face and apply
     makeup?
The sound of the cuckoo's call urges one home;
Countless multitudes of flowers have fallen, yet the
     cuckoo's call is not stilled;
Going further into the jumbled peaks, in deep
     places its call continues.

(Powell, The Record of Tung-shan)

For whom do you bathe and make yourself
    presentable?
The voice of the cuckoo urges you to come home;
Hundreds of flowers fall, yet the voice is not stilled;
Even deep in jumbled peaks, it is calling clearly.

                  (Aitken, *The Morning Star*)

S*UBMISSION* IS A TERM that carries both negative and positive connotations. To be held in submission, for instance, isn't something we typically desire. To submit to a course of training, by contrast, might carry a feeling of alignment and empowerment. As the title of this second Kokun Goi, submission means to submit to the Buddha Way and, in particular, to the practice of letting go of attachments and dualistic thoughts.

This rank's title is also translated as "serving." We serve our most honored nature by forgetting ourselves in service to all beings and by casting off attachments to images of self. We also serve the most honored nature of others by identifying everyone and all things as ourselves.

Not-knowing is a kind of submission. In three tenets practice of the Zen Peacemakers, not-knowing trains you to continually set aside fixed points of view. Not-knowing leads to a flash of openness or a sudden shift to being present in the moment. This dropping away of the things you have relied on for a sense of stability may lead you to reexamine what you believe is your center.

As Roshi Egyoku Nakao wrote, "In a world of instability, not-knowing allows us to take shelter in that empty place before anything arises, a place of emptiness and profound silence, a place of the deepest rest where self-interest has not yet entered."[1]

In the following quote from *Shobogenzo*, "Gyobutsu Igi" ("Awesome Presence of Active Buddhas"), Dogen uses the word *surrender* to refer to this experiential territory of sub-mission or not-knowing:

> Thoroughly practicing, thoroughly clarifying, is
> not forced. It is just like recognizing the shadow of
> deluded thought and turning the light around to
> shine within. The clarity of clarity beyond clarity
> prevails in the activity of buddhas. This is totally
> surrendering to practice. To understand the mean-
> ing of totally surrendering, you should thoroughly
> investigate mind. In the steadfastness of thorough
> investigation, all phenomena are the unadorned clar-
> ity of mind.

Surrender means to yield oneself to the authority of another. It is a deliberate or willful act. Instead of surrendering, we could continue to struggle or fight. But in terms of our prac-tice, we are surrendering to the authority of the Buddha and our Zen ancestors. We reach a point where their teachings start to resonate for us. If we follow Dogen's advice that surrender means to thoroughly investigate one's mind, we begin to see how grasping after our own opinions has given rise to our own suffering. With that insight, the best strategy is to submit or surrender.

Even the Buddha had to surrender when he was pur-suing his practice to eliminate suffering. When he seated himself beneath the Bodhi tree prior to his enlightenment experience, he made the following resolve: "Let only skin, sinew and bone remain, let the flesh and blood dry in my body, but I will not give up this seat without attaining complete awakening."[2] That was his complete surrender.

A monk once asked Tozan, "What does submission mean?"

Tozan said, "What did you mean when you turned your back?"

What kind of submission is it when you turn your back and pretend not to see so you can avoid getting involved? If you ignore the issue or the problem, it won't go away. But if you turn your back on your ego-grasping consciousness, you are submitting to the reality of life as it is. In this dialogue, turning your back has the implication of letting go.

The title of this rank also has the implication of "letting go." There are some things you can let go easily, while others are more difficult. Letting go of the thoughts and feelings through which you identify as an ego or a self-contained self is the most difficult.

The road to the true self is not for the weak of heart, not even for the casual meditator. Those who are just curious will be quickly disappointed. There has to be a deep longing in your heart and a fire burning in your gut. You must be willing to plunge into the abyss of the unknown, and you must be willing to surrender control to something larger than your fragmented ego. This second Kokun Goi points to a state in which you have absolutely no control. Yet surrender is not passive. It is an intentional giving up of the ego-grasping self.

There is a Zen saying: "Let go of your hold on the cliff, die completely, and then come back to life—after that you cannot be deceived." After letting go and coming back again, you live a very ordinary life in a most extraordinary way.

Surrender means you know in every fiber of your being that there is no one here living this life. Yet there is life flowing though the body-heart-mind personality for as long as it lasts. There is "no self," and that "no self" is walking, talking, working, and playing.

Back in early spring of 1972, I attended a seven-day sesshin at a home for retired Catholic nuns in Litchfield, Connecticut. The sesshin leader was Eido Shimano, whom we called Tai-san, and my first teacher, Sochu Roshi, was also there. The Litchfield sesshin was my first seven-day sesshin. I had sat for five days with Sochu Roshi but had not sat still for the entire time. When the bell rang, signaling the beginning of this sesshin, I made the following resolve: "I will not fidget, change my position, or move during any sitting period for these seven days." That was my vow of complete surrender, but Tai-san did not make it easy.

In the morning, we would get up at 4 a.m. and join a line of meditating walkers who followed a path in the nunnery along the stations of the cross. It did not escape me that I was walking up Mount Calvary to my own crucifixion.

The length of the sitting periods was pretty predictable with Sochu Roshi, just as they are at Great Mountain Zen Center. We would sit for about thirty minutes, then do walking meditation for ten minutes, then another thirty minutes of sitting, and so on. Tai-san, by contrast, varied the length of the sitting periods. Sometimes they were twenty minutes, other times they were one hundred minutes. When we sat down, we did not know when the bell would ring to signal the end of the sitting period. I felt as if I was entering Dante's Inferno: "Abandon all hope, ye who enter here." I had no option but to put myself totally into my zazen.

The zazen was strenuous much of the time. My legs and mind kept telling me to bolt and run with abandon into the snowy woods that surrounded the nunnery. But I remembered my vow not to move or fidget. At times, the body would break into a profuse sweat, or I had to grit my teeth against the pain. Then it would happen. I was suddenly floating in space with no pressure on any of my joints. My body had disappeared, and it felt like I was drifting between the stars. I was the space. I was the stars. All pain and suffering had evaporated. Where it went, I did not know, but I did not care either since I could breathe again and feel the breath pass through my body like the wind through the trees.

There was always an awareness noticing everything that was happening. That awareness reassured me that there was a huge subjective element to pain. If I could only relax and allow the pain to wash over my body, I would experience these moments of bliss more often. Who was I kidding? In the next moment, the pain would return with a vengeance. It went up and down like this for the whole seven days.

Finally, it was the last day, the last hour, and the last minute. At the end of sesshin, there was a ceremony called the Great Release, or Dai Kaijo, and indeed, it felt like a great release. I felt that the steam had escaped from the pressure cooker. Everything was light and airy and radiant.

I vividly remember the bus ride back to New York City. I noticed the new leaves on the trees, the reflection of the sun off the small streams along the way, and the billowing clouds that seemed alive. Even the noise and congestion of the city had its charm. The feeling stayed with me for days. My sesshin in Litchfield was a turning point in my life and my practice. It was my first experience of total surrender. I now knew there was no turning back. Zen was my path.

Here is Tozan's verse to interpret the second Kokun Goi:

For whom is the elaborate toilette really done?
The cuckoo's call urges the traveler to turn home.
Its note continues when myriads of flowers have
    fallen,
Calling further, deep into the intermingling peaks.

For whom is the elaborate toilette really done?

Formal Zen practice requires us to make elaborate preparations, especially for large ceremonies or extended retreats such as sesshin. You may purchase a robe or a *zafu* to create the best environment to practice zazen. Someone always prepares the flowers on the altars. Practitioners are needed to vacuum the zendo and dust the altars. Why, and for whom?

To practice at home requires preparations, too. You need to create a clean, orderly, and quiet space in which to practice. It will be a reflection of your mind during zazen. If you have children at home, sometimes it is difficult. That is why it is elaborate.

This line of the verse refers to ladies of the court who bathe and put on makeup before presenting themselves to the royal court and the emperor in particular. In this case, what does "the emperor" refer to?

In the 1970s, I used to drive monthly from San Diego to the Zen Center of Los Angeles to attend sesshin. My driving companion invariably was Charlotte Joko Beck, who was my good Dharma friend. Joko and I both worked at the University of California, San Diego, and would leave right after work. In the morning, we carefully packed our car with our meditation clothes, zafus, toiletries, and anything else we might need for sesshin. It was a two-hour drive up Interstate 5 to the Zen Center. Within a few minutes of arriving at the center, the *han* (wooden block) was struck, signaling the beginning of sesshin. We would scurry from the car, pull on our meditation clothes, and hurry to the zendo. It was an elaborate preparation for the "true emperor."

Who is the "true emperor" for whom you prepare your elaborate toilette? It is better to avoid the forbidden name. Yet we have to say something. Maezumi Roshi would preface some of his bald-faced statements by saying, "It is a bit stinky to say, but . . ." So, it is a bit stinky to say, but the elaborate toilette is for the sake of bringing out our "true self."

The cuckoo's call urges the traveler to turn home.

Aitken Roshi wrote that "the voice of the cuckoo" is true nature itself. Our true nature is calling us to find our true nature.

There is another interpretation of this line. I have heard that the cuckoo's call is mournful. That if one is despondent or feeling low, the cuckoo's call gives rise to melancholy. Most people come to practice because they are feeling some kind of painful separation. It is that feeling of separation that calls us to find our long-lost home.

Submission is still one of the initial stages of practice because there remains a belief that we can turn to our long-lost home. Those of you who have engaged in Great Heart practice, as explained in my and Shinko Perez's book *The Great Heart Way*, know that you have to turn toward the cuckoo's mournful call in order to find your long-lost home.[3] Without going through the dark night of the soul or entering the dark cave of demons, you will not find the peace and comfort of your original place. When you totally penetrate into your sorrow, that dark cave of demons transforms into your long-lost home.

The longing in your heart is the cuckoo calling you home.

Each morning when you rise, ask yourself, "What do I truly desire for this day?" Do it every day and see how it evolves. You might start off with desires for your own material comfort or your amorous interests. As you look into the longing of your heart, what is the bottom line? What is the ultimate desire, the ultimate longing?

Just like when we sit zazen and reflect on the question "Who am I?" it is not long before we realize that all the superficial answers do not satisfy us. What is the deepest longing of your heart? If you keep asking that question with sincerity and conviction, the answer will unfold in time.

It is said that Zen Master Ikkyu (1394–1481), who lived in fifteenth-century Japan, was the illegitimate son of the Japanese emperor. His mother was a lady-in-waiting in the court, who was viciously ousted by the jealous empress. So Ikkyu was raised in humble surroundings. Hearing the cuckoo's call, he spent many years coming to terms with the treatment of his mother. Ikkyu was a renowned poet and wrote this poignant poem about her:

Such a refined beauty, rouged and powdered,
Even the Buddha could not resist her;
She possesses the soul of China's Jade Beauty
Yet it is in Japan that she now languishes.[4]

After his enlightenment experience upon hearing the cawing of a crow, Ikkyu's teacher Kaso made him write an enlightenment poem as was the custom:

For ten years, I was in turmoil,
Seething and angry, but now my time has come!
The crow laughs, an Arhat emerges from the filth,
And in the sunlight of Chao-yang, a jade beauty
    sings.[5]

The last line of the poem shows his reconciliation with the fate of his mother. Ikkyu was feeling angry and self-righteous until the cuckoo—or in his case, the crow—called him home. Then he was at peace. The situation did not change, but he shone the light inward and revealed beauty everywhere.

Its note continues when myriads of flowers have fallen,

The myriad flowers represent our attachments. Even when many attachments have fallen, the mournful call of the cuckoo continues. Why is that? There are still doubts and uncertainties. Things are not clear. It remains easy to get hooked by our cherished opinions.

Recent national events have shown how divided our country is. It is probably the most divided it has been since the Civil War. As a child, I and my classmates saluted the American flag every morning and recited the Pledge of Allegiance. The last line says, "with liberty and justice for all." As a nation, we cannot agree about what liberty and justice for all looks like. Some camps of people exclude liberty and justice for other camps of people. For example, the problem with Trump and the Christian fundamentalists who supported him is not their spiritual energy but the way in which he and they use that religious energy to promote separation and intolerance at home and abroad.

A friend sent me an email from Brother David Steindl-Rast, who is a Benedictine priest and peace activist, shortly after the invasion of the Capitol building on January 6, 2021. Brother David started out his letter by saying,

> Not since March 13, 1938, when Hitler invaded Austria, have I been listening to the radio with such pain. Last night, I saw the world take a dive into darkness. Yet this morning on our website—www .gratefulness.org—the randomly generated Word for the Day happened to read:

"The same pain that can blemish our personality can act as a creative force, burnishing it into an
object of delight."
—Pir Vilayat Inayat Khan

Beneficial change comes little by little. War and tyrannical
governance can silence thousands of voices in a single blow,
whereas peace, as the Muslim psychiatrist and religious
scholar Fatma Reda wisely said, "is achieved one person at a
time, through a series of friendships."[6]

It is not only governments that create and participate in
wars. Each of us has a war going on inside. Even though we
continue to drop away myriad cherished views and attachments, more remain. Even though we step forward from
the top of the hundred-foot pole into the unknown, more
hundred-foot poles remain. The mournful cry of the cuckoo
remains as long as we believe that if only the world were
perfect according to our view of the world, we would be in
our long-lost homes.

From a Buddhist perspective, we are all one body, and
rejection of any part of that body is a root cause of suffering.
From a Buddhist psychological perspective, the judgments
and projections we make on others are reflections of parts
of our own personalities that we have disowned. They are an
indication of where we need to do work on ourselves.

When we manage to release one attachment, we have to
be careful that we are not creating another attachment in its
place. Master Bankei wrote this caution:

You people try to stop your thoughts of clinging and craving from arising, and then by stopping them you divide one mind into two, as if you are pursuing something that is running away. As long as you try to deliberately stop your rising thoughts, the thought of trying to stop them wars against the continually arising thoughts themselves, and there's never an end to it.

. . . The original clinging thoughts that you were able to stop may have come to an end, but the subsequent thoughts concerned with your stopping them won't ever cease. Well, you might wonder, then what can I do to stop them? Even if suddenly, despite yourself, and wholly unawares, rage and anger should appear, thoughts of clinging and craving arise, just let them come. Don't develop them any further. Don't attach to them. Without concerning yourself about whether to stop your rising thoughts or not to stop them, just don't bother with them. And then there's nothing else they can do but stop. You can't have an argument with a fence. When there's no one there to fight with, things can't help but simply come to an end of themselves.[7]

The clouds that obscure the sun will drift away by themselves. If you try to push them away, you are creating more clouds. Empty yourself, and the cool breezes will do all the work for you.

Bankei is telling us not to engage our thoughts during meditation. A normally functioning brain is always generating thoughts. They arise and then decay. If we can ignore them, they fade away quickly. Unfortunately, thoughts can be enticing and entertaining. It requires discipline to ignore them. During my deepest periods of meditation, I realized that I could feel a thought emerging before it broke into awareness. It was like a seedling that was pushing through the earth to show itself to the sun. The earth starts to bulge over the seedling, and then it breaks through. My bodily sensation was analogous to the bulging earth over a growing seedling. The nascent thought signaled its presence to my body, and I could easily shift my attention to my breathing or koan practice without becoming distracted.

Prior to thought, myriads of flowers have fallen. Just like thoughts, attachments fall away by themselves when we don't fuss over them. This includes our attachments to being admired, loved, and appreciated.

Read these words of the eighteenth-century Japanese Zen master Torei Zenji:

Even though someone may be a fool, be warm and
compassionate toward him. If by any chance he
should turn against us, and become a sworn enemy,
and abuse and persecute us, we should sincerely
bow down with humble language in reverent belief
that he is the merciful avatar of Buddha who uses
devices to emancipate us from sinful karma that has
been produced and accumulated upon ourselves by

our own egoistic delusion and attachment through countless cycles of time.[8]

Now that is radical, isn't it?

Calling further, deep into the intermingling peaks.

There is only one secret teaching of Zen, and I am going to share it with you right now: *Just keep going.* Vow to penetrate further into your practice to clarify your life as the enlightened life. Even in the most difficult circumstances, when you feel isolated due to the malice of others, when you feel misunderstood by your family members, when you feel the pain of the violence and intolerance in the world, the cuckoo is calling you to go further into the intermingling peaks. Not just any peaks, but the peaks that interact with other peaks, that overlap other peaks, that support other peaks. If you keep making the right effort to function from that original place, that true self, then you will act more and more appropriately to each situation.

There's a wonderful story about a very simple monk who overheard some other monks talking about enlightenment. He very much wanted to get in on their secret and told them so. They responded that first he had to prepare a meal for them, and then they would tell him. After the meal, they told him to sit in one corner of the room, and they bounced a ball off his head. They said, "Now you have achieved the first stage of arhatship." Then they put him in another corner, bounced a ball off his head, and said, "Now you have received the second stage." They did this in all four corners of the room, and by the time they got to the fourth corner, he had in fact genuinely experienced a profound enlightenment. Just because of his sincerity, his innocence, his openness, and his willingness to surrender, he opened his Zen eye. He was willing to be stupid, willing to fail, willing to be vulnerable, willing to submit. The other monks thought they were fooling him, but he was fooling them.

When children are learning how to walk, if they had any awareness of what it meant to fail, they would never learn. They are constantly falling down. Sometimes they fall down and hit parts of themselves hard on the floor, a door, a table, or what-have-you. They cry for a while, and then they get up and do it again. A wonderful lesson from little babies: they just don't give up.

There is a saying: "The one thousand failures become the success." Without those one thousand failures, there can't be success. This reminds me of a well-known quote by Einstein: "In order to be successful, the scientist has to be willing to grope in the dark for many years." Being foiled at every turn. Having no success. Just be willing to do that. Of course, using the words *success* and *failure* is kind of a funny way to talk about Zen practice. If you are trying to attain something, right there your practice has gone off course. That is because you do not know what it is that you are trying to attain. You are grasping at flowers hanging in the air. Don't cling to anything. Just let go of your cherished opinions.

Isan's enlightenment came at a time when he was working as a *tenzo* (head cook) under Hyakujo. Hyakujo asked him if the fire was still burning, and Isan went and sifted through the ashes and returned to say that it was out. Then Hyakujo went and looked even more closely and found one little burning ember. He picked it up and said, "What do you call this?" That opened Isan's eye.[9]

Just as the cuckoo is calling you further, deep into the intermingling peaks, Hyakujo was calling Isan to search deeper in the cold ash and find the burning ember. Going deep into the intermingling peaks means never giving up, to keep going no matter the weather. If the way is blocked by snow, you might need to wait for the spring thaw. But always keep your focus on the path. If you fall into the weeds, your teacher and your spiritual friends will help guide you further, deep into the intermingling peaks.

And still, the cuckoo's call urges the traveler to return home.

o   o   o   o   o

PRACTICE QUESTION

Relating to your meditation practice, what does submission or surrender mean to you? Can you apply it to your life?

11

Third Kokun Goi

Achievement or Awakening

The flowering of a withered log heralds an eternal
    spring.
Hunting a unicorn, a man rode backward on a jade
    elephant.
Now he dwells alone beyond a thousand peaks,
Blessed with bright moonshine and pure breezes.
(Luk, Ch'an and Zen Teaching)

The blooming of flowers on a sear old tree, a spring
    outside of kalpas;
Riding backward on a jade elephant, chasing the
    ch'i lin.
Now hidden far beyond the innumerable peaks,
The moon is white, the breeze cool at the approach
    of sunrise.
(Powell, The Record of Tung-shan)

Flowers bloom on a withered tree in a spring
    beyond kalpas;

You ride a jade elephant backward, chasing a winged
   dragon-deer;
Now as you hide far beyond innumerable peaks—
The white moon, a cool breeze, the dawn of a fortunate day.

                              (Aitken, *The Morning Star*)

THE THIRD KOKUN GOI is about experiencing the death of self. It is very rare. Not many have realized this state. However, dissolution of the self is not yet complete. Habits, created over many years, still have momentum and can reappear to obscure this hard-earned achievement.

Case 47 in *The Gateless Gate* is a koan called "Tosotsu's [Ch. Doushuai Congyue] Three Barriers." The third barrier is "If you are free from life and death, you know where you will go. When the four elements are decomposed, where do you go?" Until you die to your small self, you have not seen this koan or experienced this third Kokun Goi.

The name of this stage is *achievement*, but it's not meant in a self-congratulatory sense. It is more like merit or good results. I prefer the term *awakening*, which does not have a sense of gaining or losing. It emphasizes seeing clearly.

This stage is equivalent to "Catching the Ox," the fourth of the ten ox-herding pictures. Here is its description:

> After the greatest efforts the herdsman has caught
> the ox. The will is yet too obstinate and the impetus
> too strong, to break his wildness easily. At times the
> ox gets away and climbs distant plateaus. Then again
> he runs far off into deep places, filled with fog and
> clouds and wants to hide.[1]

Catching the ox can be taken as a description of an initial experience of dropping off body and mind. After dropping away body and mind, what remains? Our habit-ridden consciousness. Your habit-ridden consciousness still controls your actions in the world. You have to continue to practice and further clarify this Great Matter.

You need to work on your ingrained ways of behaving. They can be hurtful to others and to yourself because your habits are unconscious. Even seeing your true self does not mean that you can embody it or actualize it. That is why there are additional stages after this one.

When we are able to release some of our deluded thoughts and attachments, we can directly experience the world through the eyes of the Buddha, the Awakened One.

A monk asked Tozan, "What is achievement?"

Tozan said, "When throwing down a *mattock*, what is it?"

A mattock is a tool used for digging in the earth. With his answer, Tozan means when you stop all of your delusive thoughts, attachments, and inadequate activities and instead reside in nondoing, then what is it? Then you know you are endowed with the wisdom and virtue of the Buddha.

In case 15 of *The Book of Equanimity*, Isan asked Kyozan, "Where do you come from?"

Kyozan replied, "I come from the fields."

Isan asked, "How many were in the fields?"

Kyozan stuck his mattock in the ground and stood with hands folded on his chest.

Isan said, "In the southern mountains, lots of people reap thatch."

Kyozan pulled up the mattock and left.

A Zen master commented on this case, saying, "Very few understand the point of Isan's question. When Kyozan answered him by planting the hoe, buddhas and ancestors disappeared."

So, when Isan said, "How many are in the fields?" What's he really asking? Is that a Zen question or an ordinary question? Kyozan planted his mattock in the ground and crossed his arms, and in that moment, all buddhas and ancestors disappeared.

"How many were there in the fields?" Just this! Kyozan's planting the mattock in the ground represents the experience of this third Kokun Goi. Everything has dropped away, and only "Just this!" remains.

But then Isan pushes him further. He says, "Well, maybe that's so, but in the southern mountains, lots of people reap thatch. How about all the people other than 'just this'?"

Kyozan is saying it's just this, just me. How many are there? There's just me in the whole world. Isan asks about all the other people, and Kyozan just picks up his hoe and leaves. Since there is no self and no other, who are the other people? Kyozan is saying there is no distinction between self and other. In our true nature, there is only one Self.

Commenting on that, another Zen teacher wrote, "Meeting on a narrow road, escape is impossible. Having come across the bridge, he walks upon the shore, for the first time realizing that the whole body is muddy and wet."[2]

Meeting on the narrow road, escape is impossible. What's the narrow road? That's when we practice, penetrate our concentration, and see that there's no self and no other. Then we cross the bridge to enter the world of suffering and confusion to liberate others. In this process, the whole body becomes muddy and wet.

We have a phrase in Zen: to be "deluded within delusion." If there's no self and no others, then who are we saving? How does the body get wet and muddy? Those are the two sides we have to understand here, and this koan is presenting them for us. There is no self, and there is no other. There is no one to save, and yet there is suffering. This is a philosophical conundrum that boxes us into a corner. Somehow we have to get over self-absorption and engage the pain in the world.

According to some sutras, the Buddha was born fully formed out of the side of his mother. He took seven steps, pointed one finger up to the heavens and one finger to the earth, and said, "Beneath heaven and above earth, I alone am the world-honored one." Although this story is certainly mythical, it informs what Kyozan is saying in response to the question of how many were in the fields: "I alone am the world-honored one." As we shall see, this phrase is not about elevating oneself above others.

But what about all the people reaping thatch? What about all the people who are suffering? What about all the people who are getting old and losing their abilities and faculties? What about all the people who are going to work every day? After you cross over the bridge, you can't help but take care of all of them. The Buddhist interpretation of "I alone" is "I am all one with everyone." Your pain is my pain.

Let us go back to Tozan. When a monk asked him, "What is achievement?" and he responded, "When throwing down a mattock, what is it?"—was he referring to Kyozan sticking his mattock in the ground? In that case, all buddhas and ancestors and one's own self disappear. There is only just this. Or was Tozan saying that when you throw away all of your attachments, what is it? Ultimately, these two interpretations are no different.

Here is Tozan's verse for this third Kokun Goi:

> The flowering of a withered tree heralds an eternal
> spring.
> Hunting a unicorn, a man rode backward on a jade
> elephant.
> Now he hides himself higher beyond a thousand
> peaks,
> Blessed with bright moonshine and pure breezes.

The flowering of a withered tree heralds an eternal spring.

"A withered tree" refers to forgetting the self. Dying to your small self is an omen that your life will flower and reveal the wholesomeness that always has been and always will be. To forget the self is to be enlightened by all things—that is the "eternal spring." A withered tree, all its leaves fallen, symbolizes maturity in practice. There is another aspect of a withered tree: the sun can shine through and illuminate everything beneath it.

There are many references to withered plants in Zen literature. For instance, "When the grass is withered, the eagle's eye is swift." In other words, when everything drops away, then the eagle can really see clearly. It can see all the prairie dogs. When there's tall grass, it can't see them too well. If you let go of all your attachments, all of the grass in your mind withers. Then your eye sees clearly.

Case 3 in *The Transmission of Light* (also recorded in *Gateless Gate*, case 22) is about the Second Indian Ancestor, Ananda. He asked Venerable Kasyapa, "Elder Dharma brother, did the World-honored one transmit anything else to you besides the golden brocade robe?"

Kasyapa called, "Ananda!"

Ananda replied, saying, "Yes, sir."

Kasyapa said, "Knock down the flag pole in front of the gate."

Ananda was greatly awakened.

Before we appreciate this case, let's appreciate the life of Ananda.

Ananda was born the same night the Buddha realized enlightenment. He was also the Buddha's cousin. His name means "Joy," and according to Keizan Zenji, who wrote *The Transmission of Light*, everyone who saw Ananda was filled with joy.

At the age of twenty, Ananda became the Buddha's attendant and served in that capacity for twenty years until the Buddha died. He is said to have had a tremendous memory and could recall all of the Buddha's sermons.

Even though Ananda could repeat all of the Buddha's teachings, he was not enlightened, and so his case is evidence that the Way does not depend on erudition and intellectual understanding. Manifesting wisdom or embodying it is the most difficult part of our practice.

When the Buddha died, Ananda became the attendant of Kasyapa, the successor to the Buddha, and served him for twenty more years. That is when the present case took place, and Ananda would have been about sixty years old at the time.

I always find Ananda encouraging, since he spent decades attending to the original teacher and then to the First Buddhist Ancestor, yet he had not attained the Way until the event described in this case. He kept at it; he did not give up. He may have been discouraged, but he kept at it. I am sure all of us get discouraged in our practice at certain times. We start looking around for other distractions. But it always comes back to our zazen and how to bring our understanding into our lives.

Since Ananda had not realized his true self despite knowing all the public teachings, he concluded that the Buddha's ultimate teachings must have been secret. As you know, if there is anything secret, it is within you. Just look inside and discover the ancient truths. Kasyapa called Ananda, and Ananda responded. What is more natural and perfect than that? There is nothing secret in calling and responding. It is the genuine functioning of the True Self.

In ancient times, monasteries would stage Dharma combats, wherein monks would challenge their understanding of the Dharma with other monks. Each participant raised a flag, and when the winner was decided, his flag remained aloft, and the one who was defeated lowered his flag. Also, when a teacher gave a Dharma talk, the flag was raised; when the talk was over, the flag was lowered. So, when Kasyapa said, "Knock down the flag pole in front of the gate," he was indicating that the debate was complete, the discussion over. You might wonder, "Who won and who lost?" There is no winning or losing. When Kasyapa calls, the entire universe calls. When Ananda replies, the whole universe replies. It has nothing to do with secret or public.

Here is Keizan's verse for Ananda in *The Transmission of Light*:

Wisteria withered, trees fallen, mountains
  crumbled—
Valley streams gush forth and sparks pour out from
  the stones.

Let go. Let go. Keep letting go, and then become powerful and free.

Hunting a unicorn, a man rode backward on a jade elephant.

In this line, the unicorn could represent your true nature. But since a unicorn is a chimera or a fabrication of the mind, it could represent anything that is illusory. Riding backward is an act of freedom. Have you ever seen a jade elephant that you can ride? That is also an act of freedom. So, there you are looking for something that does not exist while riding backward on an immobile object. At least that is what it looks like from the outside. What does it look like from the inside?

The following miscellaneous koans give a good sense of this line:

Take a nine-story pagoda from a teapot.

Take Mount Everest from your sleeve.

Likewise, this one from *The Song of the Jewel Mirror Samadhi*:

> The wooden man starts to sing, the stone woman
>   gets up dancing.
> It is not attained in thought or feelings, so how to
>   reflect on it?

How free is that? It is even better than the gingerbread man.

Tozan's line about hunting a unicorn while riding backward on a jade elephant has an air of playfulness. It is akin to the court jester who acts like a fool but displays a candor that cuts through the false posturing of those in the court.

When Ikkyu was a novice monk, he kept exposing the hypocrisy of the abbot. The abbot was fond of sweets and kept a jar in his quarters. He warned Ikkyu and the other temple boys, "This candy is beneficial for adults, but if a child eats it, he will die immediately." As soon as the abbot was away, Ikkyu took all of the candy and shared it with the other boys. He then broke one of the tea bowls in the abbot's room. When the abbot returned, Ikkyu went to the abbot in tears and said, "While cleaning your honored room, I accidentally broke this precious bowl. To make amends for this terrible deed, I swallowed some of the poisoned candy. Nothing happened, so I took all of it to make sure that I would die. Unfortunately, I did not, so please forgive me."

Ikkyu used shock tactics on one of the temple's wealthy patrons who was fond of leather clothing, which at the time was considered inappropriate garb for Buddhists. When the patron approached, he saw a sign that was written by Ikkyu's hand: "Leather goods are not allowed on temple grounds. Those who break this rule will be severely beaten."

The patron was furious and stormed in to confront Ikkyu, demanding, "What about the big drum in the main hall? Isn't it covered with leather?"

Ikkyu said, "Yes it is true. But then we beat it soundly morning and night. If you insist on wearing leather, you will get the same treatment."[3]

When Roshi Bernie Glassman felt that his colleagues and students were getting too serious or taking themselves and their rituals too seriously, he sought out a clown with whom to study clowning methods. He started to wear a red nose at important meetings to lighten the atmosphere. Then he founded the Order of Disorder to promote humor, fun, and love. Those in the order even have their own five ranks:

1. Disorder found
2. Honoring the disorder in your life
3. Getting real—getting in touch with the disorder in your life
4. Mutual deterioration
5. Disorder attained

To many outsiders, Zen practice and practitioners seem to be strict, rigid, and serious. Tozan captures the playfulness of Zen with this line of his verse. To catch a unicorn while riding backward on a jade elephant is the height of freedom.

Now he hides himself higher beyond a thousand peaks,

How do you hide yourself higher beyond a thousand peaks? There is no Buddha above and no beings below. There is no self to grab. Since it is all one body, where is the small ego-grasping self?

In case 64 of *The Book of Equanimity*, Zen Master Hogen said, "Among the myriad forms is a solitary, manifest body. Does it wipe out the myriad forms, or does it not wipe out the myriad forms?"

When he hides himself higher beyond a thousand peaks, do they wipe out himself? Or does he wipe out the thousand peaks? Or are they both wiped out simultaneously?

Our brains think in a dualistic way. They store ideas and concepts. Then the ego becomes attached to these various ideas and concepts. Those attachments are what keep us from seeing the interconnectedness of life. So, the practices of Zen help us to become nonattached to those ideas. It doesn't mean you don't have ideas; it means you're not attached to them.

If you can let go of those attachments, then you can experience the connectedness and inter-relational characteristics of life. That's what Buddhism is about.

The ten thousand things are one body. What is that one body? It's not enough to be one with the absolute. You're not just the absolute. You're everything together. When subject and object vanish, who are you? When box and lid join perfectly, there is no discernible seam. When absolute and relative interpenetrate, there is no gap. Yet in this third Kokun Goi, awakening, the practitioner is not able to sustain this state of mind and slips back into a notion of self that is separate from the ten thousand peaks.

As mentioned in chapter 2, the great master Gensha used to say, "The entire universe is one bright pearl." No matter what comes up, it is the complete working of freedom. It is only our ideas, beliefs, images, and projections that obscure that fact.

As long as we feel that we can escape from the present situation, we won't notice very much about our ego-grasping mind. Only when we feel that "this is it" and there is no escape will our perceptions, feelings, and intelligence really come alive. This particularly pertains to zazen during sesshin or to bearing witness retreats. Just totally surrender to it.

Master Hogen asked, "Among the myriad forms is solitary manifest body. Does it wipe out the myriad forms, or does it not wipe out the myriad forms?"

When you realize that boundless, luminous self-nature that is no nature, does it obscure all of the myriad forms, all of the ingredients that make up your life? If you say yes, it is a duality. If you say no, it is a duality.

Nonetheless, if you manifest the solitary body and experience freedom in the dark cave of demons, then the appropriate action will present itself.

Blessed with bright moonshine and pure breezes.

The enlightened life is to be blessed no matter what occurs. It includes joy and pain. Every day is a good day, even when you are having difficulties. Faithfully follow the example of the Buddha, and you will be blessed with bright moonshine and pure breezes.

Case 96 of *The Book of Equanimity* relates the following:

While Kyuho was at Master Sekiso's monastery, he became Sekiso's attendant. When Sekiso passed away, the assembly wanted to appoint the head monk of the meditation hall as chief priest. Kyuho did not approve, and so said, "Wait until I question him. If he understands our late master's intent, I will serve him as I did our late master."

Then he asked the head monk, "Our late master said, 'Go through, desist, cease. One thought is ten thousand years. Cold ashes and withered trees, and one strip of pure white silk.' Tell me, what state of affairs does this clarify?"

The head monk said, "It clarifies the affair of a one-colored state."

Kyuho said, "If that is so, you do not quite understand our late master's intent."

The head monk said, "Don't you approve of me? Prepare incense and bring it to me."

Kyuho did so and then, burning the incense, the head monk declared, "If I did not understand our late master's intent, I won't be able to expire while the incense is still burning." So saying, he sat down and died.

Kyuho patted him on the back, saying, "It's not that you can't expire while sitting or pass away while standing. It's just that you haven't seen our late master's intent, even in your dreams."

The head monk was stuck in this stage of achievement. You might be able to enter deep samadhi and even develop special psychic abilities. That is not sufficient. How are you going to function in the world? The functioning of wisdom is compassion. If you still hang on to your habit-ridden consciousness of having to be superior to others, of knowing more than others and knowing what is best, then you might as well expire while sitting and pass away while standing. You still won't know our late master's intent, even in a dream.

Here's what Isan had to say about that: "If a person is truly enlightened, and has realized the fundamental, and is aware of it himself, in such a case, he is actually no longer tied to the poles of cultivation and non-cultivation." In other words, he no longer has to worry about whether enlightenment is sudden or gradual, which was the point of active debate at that time.

Isan continued, "However, ordinarily, even though the original mind has been awakened by an intervening cause, so that the person is instantaneously enlightened in his reason and spirit, yet there remains the inertia of habit, formed since the beginning of time, which cannot be totally eliminated at a stroke. He must be taught to cut off completely the streams of habitual ideas and views caused by the still operative Karmas."[4]

Of course, the koan involving Kyuho and the head monk is not about being able to die at will or possess other incredible powers like having wild animals eat out of your hand, being able to read others' minds, or being able to walk on water. That is not the point of our practice, and these things do not constitute enlightenment.

"Go through, desist, cease. One thought is ten thousand years. Cold ashes and withered trees, and one strip of pure white silk." Sekiso's phrases are similar to the Kokun Goi in their progression. Whatever obstacles come up, just keep going through—particularly, go through all the other stages of practice. Desist holding on to your ignorance. Cease thinking that you're something because you let go of your ego-grasping mind!

"One thought is ten thousand years." Whether large or small, yesterday or tomorrow, each thing does not fail to completely cover the ground. Everything is contained in this very moment. In their life cycle, cattle ticks drop off their host animal, climb a blade of grass and wait for another animal to pass. Then they jump on the new host in order to mate and strengthen their gene pool. Studies show that a tick will wait on the blade of grass for months before it smells cattle and leaps. We can only imagine what the passage of time means for the tick. One thought, or in this case, one scent is ten thousand years.

"Cold ash and withered trees." How can you become cold ash and still have hot blood pumping through your veins? If you really drop away body and mind, that's the state of cold ash. You have no fear of death. Why not? Because you've already dropped away all of your attachments, so you can move very freely.

When Americans think of a withered tree, we think of something ugly and dead that needs to be dug up and put in the compost heap. But as we've seen, a withered tree in this case symbolizes maturity. In terms of our practice, it is not only having had experiences of awakening and seeing clearly, of having dropped away attachments, but also having matured like a fine wine, till the bouquet is just perfect.

The last item in the list is "one strip of pure white silk." Yasutani Roshi used to encourage his students to be like a clean sheet of white paper—uncluttered, totally available to be drawn on. It's like a mirror. A mirror will reflect anything, but it won't become tainted. One strip of pure white silk is free to be anything, according to what the situation is.

There's a Zen saying that might help you understand this rank: "When your bow is broken and your last arrow spent, then shoot! Shoot with your entire heart!" Drop away all your impediments, and just really open your heart and be right there.

Then you will be blessed with bright moonshine and pure breezes.

○　○　○　○　○

PRACTICE QUESTION

Hakuin said that a big impediment to complete awakening is our habit-ridden consciousness. When you look carefully at your unspoken beliefs and habits, what do you discover?

12

Fourth Kokun Goi

Collective Achievement or Collective Awakening

Buddhas and living beings do not hinder one
  another.
The mountain may be high and deep the water;
In the midst of contraries, clear understanding wins
  the day,
(And yet) the partridge calls among a myriad fresh
  flowers.

(Luk, Ch'an and Zen Teaching)

Ordinary beings and Buddhas have no truck with
  each other;
Mountains are naturally high, waters naturally deep.
What the myriad distinctions and numerous differ-
  ences show is that
Where the chukar cries, many flowers are blooming.

(Powell, The Record of Tung-shan)

Ordinary beings and Buddhas have no interchange;
Mountains are high of themselves; waters are deep
    of themselves.
What do the myriad distinctions and differences
    reveal?
Where the partridge calls, many flowers are
    blooming.

(Aitken, *The Morning Star*)

I N THE PREVIOUS RANK of achievement or awakening, the practitioner—despite having experienced death of the self to some extent or for some period of time—still holds on to a sense of an independent, autonomous self that stands aloof and evaluates the experience of awakening. That sense of self is conditioned by one's habits. This fourth rank is called collective achievement or collective awakening. It does not necessarily have to do with some kind of mass, simultaneous awakening—multitudes of people awakening together and creating a formidable force that marches together to create good (although that would be nice). It has more to do with identifying one's self with the collectivity of all beings, all things, and the interpenetrating relationships that make up one's life.

Put differently, it is the realization that our minds and hearts are no other than all beings everywhere—the mountains, the rivers, the plants, the animals, the Great Earth, the sun, the moon, and the stars.

Dharma Master Jo (Ch. Zhao) offered one of the classic Zen formulations of this realization when he said, "Heaven and earth have the same root. The ten thousand things are one body." (*Book of Equanimity*, case 91)

Just like heaven and earth, praise and blame have the same root. What is that root? Are you aware of the spaciousness that envelops heaven and earth, praise and blame, the mountains and the rivers? Are you aware of the silence that drowns out the judgments and projections of your mind? The container of each life is vast and empty. Our feelings, emotions, and thoughts arise within that spaciousness. Problems arise when we forget about the space and make the objects of our perception solid and immutable. What a pity!

A monk asked Tozan, "What is collective achievement?"

Tozan said, "Not attaining things." (Other translations of this line include "Not one matter" or "Nothing outside.")

Not attaining things means that you don't add anything extra. There is nothing separate from you. You are everything, without exception. So, there is nothing you can add.

In this context, the question "What can I gain from meditation?" does not make any sense. A better question is "What can I diminish through my meditation?" We can start with the three poisons of greed, hatred, and delusion. Then we can cease to cherish our opinions. Then we can forget the self.

Suzuki Roshi wrote that to make right effort in our practice means to get rid of whatever is extra.[1] Right effort means to let go of our attachments and dualistic thoughts. They only lead to suffering. Not attaining things means that we lack nothing. What remains to be sought?

Dogen Zenji, as a young man, asked, "If it is true that from the very beginning all beings are the Buddha, why is it so difficult to realize it?"[2] He was not wrong about that difficulty: When you reflect on the lives of the ancestors, the Zen masters, and even the Buddha himself, all of them went through a similar process involving a penetrating search and difficult discipline. And all of them ultimately realized that, from the very beginning, we all are the Buddha. Why did they, and why do we, have to make so much effort? If we are all the Buddha, what is all this striving?

This question became the young Dogen Zenji's very first koan. Eventually, his pursuit of this question took him all the way to China—a very difficult, sometimes life-threatening journey in the thirteenth century. There he met his Dharma teacher, Tendo Nyojo, and eventually realized for himself the answer to this question. Dogen Zenji pointed out that the basic contradiction between our inherent Buddha Nature and our incessant sense of struggle occurs when we view reality, our lives, from our small, clinging, discriminating minds. From the perspective, or more accurately, the *experience* of collective awakening, the contradiction appears ridiculous because it is nonexistent.

Buddha said, "I and all beings everywhere have simultaneously attained the Way." (*The Transmission of Light*, case 1) There was no gap between the Buddha and all beings. He had totally merged, and there was not even a hair's breadth of difference.

Think of dying a piece of cloth. The dye penetrates every fiber of the cloth such that they are inseparable. You cannot discern what is dye and what is cloth.

To take another analogy, an alloy is a substance composed of two or more metals intimately united, usually by being fused together and dissolving into each other when molten. Brass, for example, is an alloy of copper and zinc. It is neither copper nor zinc. They are fused so intimately that atoms of copper are in the crystal structure of zinc and the atoms of zinc are in the crystal structure of copper. That is what "not attaining things" means—that degree of intimacy. So intimate that you do not know where you end and I begin. We transform, and there is no "small I" that has a separate identity.

In case 21 of *The Book of Equanimity*, Ummon addressed the assembly, asking, "The old Buddha and the freestanding pillar are mingled together. What level of activity is this?"

The assembly said nothing, so Ummon himself answered, "In the South Mountain clouds rise. In the North Mountain, rain falls."

The Buddha-mind is not only vast bodies like the Great Earth, the sun, the moon, and the stars; it is also the pillar that holds up the temple roof, a broken tile on the bathroom floor, and a pile of asphalt used to repair potholes in the road. When the old Buddha mingles with the freestanding pillar, he experiences no separation between himself and the pillar. When he experiences no separation between himself and the pillar, he embodies all of the joy and pain in the world. Thus, when clouds rise on the South Mountain, rain falls on the North Mountain. When someone in Africa sneezes, someone in Europe says, "Gesundheit!" When you are sad, I cry. When you say, "Thank you," I say, "You're welcome." In this way, collective awakening is realized.

As we saw in chapter 5, the Diamond Sutra says, "Dwelling in no place, raise the Bodhi mind." Not attaining things means not even having a place. It is said that there is no place like home. Let's go a step further and say no place *is* home.

"No place is home" simultaneously means every place, every aspect of yourself, and everyone you meet is home. In the process of spiritual transformation, it's crucial to treat our inner perpetrator with compassion. Saint, devil, victim, and perpetrator are just one mind. But that doesn't mean you aren't responsible for how you treat other people. The American Episcopal priest Barbara Brown Taylor wrote, "The hardest spiritual work in the world is to love the neighbor as the self—to encounter another human being not as someone you can use, change, fix, help, save, enroll, convince or control, but simply as someone who can spring you from the prison of yourself, if you will allow it."[3]

There are a few examples of what you might think of as collective awakening in Zen literature. One of the most famous is the story of the seven sisters, as recounted in Dogen's *Eihei Koroku*, discourse 64.[4] Here is my version of that story:

In India there were seven sisters from a very wealthy family. Each weekend, they gathered together for a party. One day, however, one of the sisters suggested, "Today instead of having a party, let's go to the crematory. If we do, something nice will happen."

So, they went to the crematory and saw numerous corpses. Seeing the dead people, one of them cried out, "All these corpses, where did the person go?" And from that remark, all seven sisters simultaneously attained enlightenment.

Seeing this, the god Indra was very much impressed. He descended from his heaven to talk to the sisters. "You did such a marvelous thing, and I am very impressed," he told them. "I should like to give you some reward. Anything you ask for, I will give to you."

The sisters discussed what they wanted. "Jewelry? No! We already have too many jewels. Money? We don't have to worry about that sort of thing. Clothes? We have enough."

Finally, they came up with three wishes and said to Indra, "We appreciate your offer and have decided on three things: first, we would like a tree with no root; second, we would like a piece of land where there is no yin and yang; and third, a valley in which there is no echo."

Indra said, "These are difficult things to give. In your country lives Shakyamuni Buddha. He will be able to grant you these three things that you want."

The rootless tree represents the very state of emptiness. When we human beings are completely, utterly present without a separate consciousness of being Peter or Mary or whatever our names are, we can say we are empty. We can say that we do not have eye, ear, nose, tongue, body, or mind when we are in the state of emptiness. With no eye, I see; with no ear, I hear; with no nose, I smell; with no hands, I touch. We have dropped off the concepts of body and mind. When we have dropped the boxes of concepts, we experience the real thing without constraints.

The land where there is no yin and yang is the land where dualism does not exist. We divide things into opposition all the time. We view everything as either good or bad, or it might be neutral. Always it is relative to "me." Dogen says that this land is the crematorium itself. "Where did the person go?" In the Heart Sutra, it says, "Form is emptiness. Emptiness is form." Can we see emptiness through form? Can we see form through emptiness?

The third wish of the sisters is a valley where there is no echo. Dogen's comment on this is reminiscent of the second Hensho Goi, "the absolute in the midst of the relative."

Dogen wrote, "I would call upon them, and if the seven wise sisters respond, I will say, 'I have just given you the echo of that valley.' If they do not respond, I will say, 'Indeed, there is no echo.'"[5]

Regardless of whether the sisters respond or not, fundamentally there is no echo in the valley. Fundamentally life and death are empty, and they are a marvelous thing.

How we practice is important. How much of the ego-grasping we are willing to let go of will determine how we embody these three wishes of the seven wise sisters. Our rootless tree will take hold in any soil or nonsoil. Our compass in the land without north and south will always be true. What is the original sound of a valley without echo? Speak quickly without using your tongue and lips!

Here is Tozan's verse for this fourth Kokun Goi:

> Buddhas and living beings do not hinder one
>   another.
> The mountain is high and deep the water;
> In the midst of contraries, clear understanding wins
>   the day,
> Myriad fresh flowers blooming where the partridge
>   calls.

Buddhas and living beings do not hinder one another.

There are no buddhas above and no living beings below. Everything is perfectly whole and complete as it is. It is not one-sided; there is a mutual responsibility between the student and the teacher. We are not only humans practicing to be buddhas but also buddhas practicing to be fully human.

When I first came to the Zen Center of Los Angeles in 1972, Maezumi Roshi had a plaque at the entrance to the zendo that read in part:

Let us be harmonious like milk dissolved in water.

Temporarily, there are the relationships of guests to master and juniors to seniors; however, eventually all of us will be Buddhas forever. We should maintain the Buddha-Mind, moment after moment.

Let us not waste time. Time flies swiftly and nothing is dependable. Reflect upon the transiency of our lives.

Do not blame or criticize others. Do not imitate the falsehood of others, but nourish your own virtue. Correct errors and do not hate them.

. . .

Let us be respectful to ourselves and others, as well as to the Buddha.

Our zazen is the zazen of Buddhas. Transcending both enlightenment and delusion; let us be aware of this very fact.

Let us be selfless and be ourselves and accomplish the Great Four Vows together.

Maha Prajna Paramita,

Taizan Hakuyu (Maezumi), Gassho [1968]

Father Robert Kennedy, a Jesuit priest who was empowered as a Zen roshi by Roshi Bernie Glassman, likes to tell this story of an encounter with Maezumi Roshi. Father Kennedy was working on this koan from case 7 of *The Blue Cliff Record*:

A monk asked Master Hogen, "I am Echo. What is the Buddha?"

Hogen said, "You are Echo."

As Father Kennedy was floundering around with this koan, Maezumi Roshi suddenly bellowed at him, "You are Father Kennedy, the Buddha."

It was so obvious to Maezumi Roshi and so obscure to Father Kennedy—at that time.

I once received advice from an old Buddhist teacher to see everyone as the Buddha. What would it be like if, when you went to the grocery store, you saw everyone as the Buddha? That includes all the shoppers, all the employees stocking the shelves, the cashiers, the pharmacist, the butchers, the bakers, and the candlestick makers. How about when you are driving your car? Can you see all the other drivers as the Buddha? What about your partner, your boss, or your coworkers? Everywhere you look there is Buddha, both inside and outside. Hakuin said, "This very body is the body of Buddha."[6]

The mountain is high and deep the water;

Ducks have short legs; flamingos have long legs. I am old; my granddaughter is young. What is the problem?

Dogen wrote in *Shobogenzo*, "Genjokoan":

When the need is large, it is used largely.
When the need is small, it is used in a small way.
Thus, no creature ever comes short of its own
   completeness.
Wherever it stands, it does not fail to cover the
   ground.

Even an ant does not fail to completely cover the ground. Everything is just as it is and need not be otherwise.

A monk once asked Baso, "Your reverence, abandoning the four propositions and wiping out the one hundred negations, please point out to me directly the meaning of Bodhidharma's coming from the West."

Baso said, "I don't feel like explaining to you today. Go ask Chizo (Ch. Xitang Zhizang)."

The monk then went to ask Chizo, and Chizo said, "Why don't you ask the master?"

The monk said, "The master told me to ask you."

Rubbing his head with his hand, Chizo said, "I've got a headache today. Go and ask Brother Kai (Jp. Hyakujo Ekai; Ch. Baizhang Huaihai)."

The monk asked Kai, and Kai said, "Since coming here, I don't know."

The monk returned and asked Baso what had happened, and Baso said, "Chizo's head is white, Kai's head is black." (*Book of Equanimity*, case 6)

Four propositions and one hundred negations—what are those? The four propositions are oneself, others, being, and nonbeing. The hundred negations expand from these four propositions and get quite elaborate. The propositions and negations are based on Buddhist logic that was expounded to destroy the delusive thoughts we have about reality. Whole libraries have been written on these topics, so basically, the monk is asking, "Leaving aside all of the Buddhist philosophy and cosmology, what is the ultimate truth of Zen?"

Baso said, "I don't feel like explaining it today." Right there, he's explaining it. To truly practice, we must abandon the four propositions and wipe out the hundred negations. In fact, at some point, we must let go of everything that is created by thoughts. But the monk doesn't get it. How can we hold the four propositions and hundred negations without solidifying it into true and false, or right and wrong? That's why we sit, to bring our awareness to each of the obstacles we create for ourselves.

"Chizo's head is white, Kai's head is black." Chizo has his way of behaving, and Kai has his way of behaving. We are not the same, and yet we are the same.

The sky is blue; the grass is green. Dogs bark; cats meow. Ducks have ducklings; geese have goslings. Why do we make it so complicated?

I'm a cis male, and my wife is a cis female. Where are the four propositions and the hundred negations in that? We always want to add something extra to create the illusion of control, safety, and security.

Life completely penetrates each of us. Large and small do not come close to expressing it. Everyone has the wisdom and virtue of the Buddha Tathagata.

In the midst of contraries, clear understanding wins the day,

How does one clarify the ten thousand differences?

In chapter 1, I mentioned a monk's question that appears in case 100 of *The Book of Equanimity*. The monk asked Kaku Osho of Roya, "If the original state is clean and pure, then why suddenly do rivers, mountains, and the Great Earth arise?"

Kaku replied, "If the original state is clean and pure, then why suddenly do the mountains, rivers, and Great Earth arise!"

Kaku Osho of Roya studied with Fumyo Zensho (Ch. Wude Shanzhao) and eventually became his successor. During one winter training period, Fumyo Zensho stopped the night zazen because it was so bitterly cold that everybody was having a difficult time. One day, when he was in his quarters trying to keep warm, an Indian monk arrived there flying on a cloud, and he begged the master not to waste the time. He said, "Though this congregation is not large, six of them are great vessels, and their path will give shelter to humans." So, the very next day, Fumyo continued the schedule. One of those six is the famed master in this case, Kaku Osho of Roya.

Sometimes it is hot in the zendo at my temple, and sometimes it is cold. We try to add heat in the winter and cold air in the summer, so it has never become so bitterly cold or so swelteringly hot that I have considered stopping the schedule. When Hakuin inherited his teacher's temple near his hometown of Hara, it was in such bad repair that you could see the stars through the roof. When it rained, he had to carry a raincoat from his abbot's quarters to the zendo. We Zen practitioners today are so fortunate.

In this case, the monk asked, "If the original state is clean and pure, then why suddenly do rivers, mountains, and the Great Earth arise?" That question comes from a scripture in which one of the disciples of the Buddha, Varuna, asked, "If all the faculties and sense data in the world, the life clusters, the sense media, and elements of sense and consciousness and so forth, are all the mind of realization and suchness, pure in its original state, why does it suddenly produce mountains, rivers, earth, and all the compounded characteristics that gradually change in flux, end, and then begin again?" As was typical of the movement of Buddhism from India to China, the Chinese monk distilled this question into a simpler form than its elaborate Indian presentation.

Roya just repeated the monk's words—if the original state is clean and pure, how does it suddenly produce rivers, mountains, and earth! In Zen, we call this type of response "mounting the bandit's horse to chase the bandit." In the mouth of the monk, these words are a question. In Roya's mouth, they become an exclamation. The original state is pure! Mountains and rivers suddenly appear!

So, what's the problem? The problem is that when painful or uncomfortable situations or feelings arise, we think they're not pure. The truth is they're neither pure nor impure. They just are.

In case 23 of *The Gateless Gate*, the Sixth Ancestor said, "Think neither good nor evil. At such a moment what is your original face?" The Sixth Ancestor's statement could be taken as an exclamation identical in spirit to Roya's. When you think neither good nor evil, the original state is pure. That is your true self! Mountains and rivers suddenly appear!

A student once asked a Zen master, "My wisdom is tightly confined within me, but I am unable to make use of it! How can I use it?" (At least he admits it's within him!)

The master said, "My friend, come closer!"

When the student came a few steps closer, the master said, "How wonderfully well you're using it!"

We use it all the time. If our wisdom is tightly bound inside us, how do we use it? If the original state is clean and pure, then why do the mountains, rivers, and the Great Earth suddenly arise? Just cease to cherish your opinions and let it function freely.

Myriad fresh flowers blooming where the partridge calls.

This line is reminiscent of case 24 of *The Gateless Gate*:

A monk asked Fuketsu (Ch. Fengxu Yanzhao), "How can we transcend both speech and silence?"

Fuketsu said, "I constantly think of Konan in March, where the partridges sing among hundreds of sweet-scented blossoms."

The partridge is the most beloved songbird. Its call reminds one of joyous occasions and true love. By contrast, the cuckoo, evoked in the second Kokun Goi, makes a mournful sound.

This fourth stage is the comingling of the absolute and the relative. Even though we see the flowers and hear the

THE FIVE RANKS OF THE SEQUENCE OF MERIT

partridge, there is no fixed place on which to stand. Abiding in no place, raise the mind that manifests one's enlightenment and that of others.

Here is the verse from case 55 of *The Book of Equanimity* (Seppo the rice cook):

Within the group there's a guest from Konan.
Don't sing the partridge's song before men.

When we hear the song of the partridge, we recall pleasant times and disengage from life instead of just hearing the partridge call. So Wanshi wrote, "Don't sing the partridge song before men," meaning don't tempt others to fall into fantasies. They forget that flowers fall though we love them. Weeds sprout though we hate them. That is just life itself.

When we don't honor everything, it leads to waste through sloppiness and greed. In Japan, there is an annual memorial service by seamstresses for all the needles they've broken during the year. When a zafu (meditation cushion) is out of place, do you use your foot to adjust it, or do you take a moment to bend over and use your hands? When you hit a bell, do you bring out its best quality, or do you hit it so hard that it screams in pain or so softly that it ignores you? How do you treat a piece of broken tile or an odd-shaped piece of drywall?

No creature, whether sentient or insentient, ever comes short of its own completeness. Wherever it stands, it does not fail to cover the ground.

○   ○   ○   ○   ○

PRACTICE QUESTION

What are you rejecting in your life that, if you were able to clarify it and accept it, would relieve your suffering? What are you holding on to that, if you could see its transient nature, would relieve your suffering?

13

Fifth Kokun Goi

Absolute Achievement or Absolute Awakening

The rearing up the head's horn shows its
   unworthiness.
A mind set on the quest of Buddhahood is shameful
   indeed!
Since the far distant empty eon—no one yet has
   known
That which journeyed south to visit fifty-three
   sages.

> (Luk, *Ch'an and Zen Teaching*)

Can't stand head sprouting horns anymore;
When the mind rouses to seek the Buddha, it's time
   for compunction (*penitence*).
In the unimpeded vista of the Kalpa of Emptiness,
   when no one is perceived,
Why go south in search of the fifty-three?

> (Powell, *The Record of Tung-shan*)

When head and horns peep out, it no longer
    endures;
If you arouse your mind to seek Buddha, it's time
    for compunction;
In the Kalpa of Emptiness, there is no one who
    knows;
Why go to the South to interview fifty-three sages?

(Aitken, *The Morning Star*)

I N THE FIFTH RANK, absolute achievement, all traces of self and enlightenment vanish. This is complete liberation.

This stage corresponds to the tenth ox-herding picture, "Entering the Market with Open Hands." Its description states, "With bare chest and feet, he enters the market. His face is smeared with earth, his head covered with ashes. A huge laugh streams over his cheeks. Without humbling himself to perform miracles or wonders, he suddenly makes the withered trees bloom."[1]

This paragraph depicts Hotei, who is sometimes called the Laughing Buddha. He has a big belly and an infectious smile, and he carries a sack over his shoulder from which he gives people what they want—not what he thinks they need. He is free to be who he is without constraints or inhibitions. His mission is to bring insight and happiness to everyone he meets.

Consider carefully the following verse. It encapsulates the fifth Kokun Goi:

> If one understands how to meet one's own self and
> yet to remain unknown to the self—the gate to
> the palace will open wide.

This represents your life as it is, not as you imagine it is. Because we want our lives to be other than they are, we cannot just accept them as they are. Going beyond achievement, nothing extra needs to be added or subtracted. If we see our lives clearly and have a right attitude, the gate to the palace will open wide.

A monk asked Tozan, "What is absolute achievement?"

Tozan replied, "Nothing shared."

"Nothing shared" means that all traces of self and other have disappeared. Furthermore, there is no inside and no outside, so there is nothing to share. If everything is one, what is there to share? Even the concept of "collective" no longer makes sense.

There is a verse in case 85 of *The Book of Equanimity* about the National Teacher's Seamless Monument, which describes this rank:

South of Sho and north of Tan,
yellow gold within fills the whole country.
A ferry boat under the shadowless tree.
In the crystal palace, there is no one who knows.

"South of Sho and north of Tan" means all of China. Sho is in the north, and Tan is in the south. In this case, it means everywhere in the ten directions.

"Yellow gold fills the whole country." Have you heard the expression "the Golden Buddha"? Due to the luster and radiance of his skin, the historical Buddha was often referred to as the Golden Buddha. Many statues of the Buddha, especially in Thailand, are crafted from pure gold. So, you can imagine that yellow gold filling the whole country could mean that this Golden Buddha is everywhere. Or Buddha

Nature is everywhere. It does not miss any spot, even the end of your toenail.

"A ferry boat under a shadowless tree" takes children, men, women, and people of all genders from the shore of samsara to the shore of nirvana. The shadowless tree is essential; otherwise, the ferry conductor would not know where to go. This tree illuminates the route. It is the awakened state itself.

The last line directly answers the monk's question, "What is absolute achievement?" (Other translations are "What is accomplishment of accomplishment?" and "What is absolute awakening?") "In the crystal palace, there is no one who knows." A crystal palace is transparent. Nothing is hidden. And yet, there is no one who knows. With complete understanding, what is there to know? Dogs bark, and ducks quack. What is there to know? Bow wow, quack, quack. Each is complete. Ducks have no calling to bark, and dogs have no urge to quack. There is nothing shared. Just bow wow. Just quack, quack.

The twentieth-century Japanese Zen master Uchiyama Roshi said, "The true Self has nothing to do with 'others'; it is a Self that lives totally within itself. The world as experienced is the world which the Self alone, you alone, can experience. . . . When you are born, your world is born with you, and when you die, so does your entire world. Your true Self includes the entire world you live in, and in this world there is no possibility of exchange."

Thus Tozan said, "Nothing shared."

Uchiyama concludes, "The 'world' is not some entity which exists apart from us; the 'world' is where we function. Likewise, the life of the true Self is not some entity apart from our functioning and working. Everything we encounter is our life."[2]

Are we to take Uchiyama Roshi's words to mean we are truly completely separate from other people and living in a world that is different from theirs? First, Uchiyama Roshi says each of us is completely alone, and any exchange between us, even trading a fart, is impossible. However, at the end of his statement, he says, "Everything we encounter is our life."

This means we are everyone and everything we encounter. There are no others, and there is no separation between either self and other, subject and object, or sense organs and objects of the sense organs. It seems that the beginning and the end of Uchiyama Roshi's statement are completely opposite and contradictory. It is important to clearly see this apparent contradiction. Is it really a contradiction, or is Uchiyama saying the same thing in two different ways? Once we have experienced realization of our true nature, we can move seamlessly between these positions.

In *Shobogenzo*, "Zenki" ("Total Function of Life and Death"), Dogen wrote, "The ultimate goal of Buddhism is detachment from, that is total immersion in, life and death."

So Dogen is saying that "detachment from" and "total immersion in" are the same thing. Do Dogen's words resolve Uchiyama's apparent contradiction? When you experience no separation in any aspect of your life, there is nothing to share and no one to share with. Yet since we are all one, we are immersed in all the joy and pain in every life.

Years ago, when we were taking walks together, my Dharma friend Joko Beck used to talk about the famous koan of Joshu's dog, wherein a monk asked Joshu, "Does a dog have Buddha Nature?"

Joshu answered "Mu!"

Mu literally means "no," but Joshu is demonstrating Buddha Nature with his exclamation of mu. The koan student has to present this mu to their teacher. All Joko could say was, "It's not this. Not this. Not this," as she pointed things out. It is not your thoughts. It is not your ideas. It is not your feelings. There is no one who knows, and yet, the student has to present mu to their teacher.

A similar Dharma dialogue occurred in the ninth century:

A monk asked Master Ikan of Kozenji (Ch. Xingshan Weikuan), "Has a dog Buddha Nature or not?"

MASTER: "Yes"

MONK: "Have you, O Master, the Buddha Nature or not?"

MASTER: "I have not."

MONK: "All sentient beings have the Buddha Nature. Why is it that you alone, Master, have not?"

MASTER: "I am not among all sentient beings."

MONK: "If you are not among all sentient beings, are you a Buddha or not?"

MASTER: "I am not a Buddha."

MONK: "What kind of thing are you after all?"

MASTER: "I am not a thing either."

MONK: "Can it be seen and thought of?"

MASTER: "Even if you try to think about it and know it, you are unable to do so. It is therefore called 'unknowable.'"[3]

Not-knowing is most intimate. This intimacy is demonstrated by Tozan's fifth Kokun Goi. It is therefore called unknowable.

Let's look at Tozan's verse for this fifth and final Kokun Goi:

Slightly rearing up the head's horn even a little is unworthy.
A mind set on the quest of Buddhahood is shameful indeed!
The far distant empty eon—no one has known it yet.
How necessary is it to journey south to visit fifty-three sages?

Slightly rearing up the head's horn even a little is unworthy.

This first line—and indeed all the lines of this verse—appears to be a negation. Each line states how things should not be. Don't rear up the head's horns. Don't seek Buddhahood. No one knows the empty kalpa. It is not necessary to seek guidance. How can we say how things should be without getting stuck in one position or another?

Referring to the source of knowledge, Nansen said, "Clearly, if you speak of it, then horns will grow on your head."[4] It is better to have nothing than to have something good. If you think you have accomplished something extraordinary, horns will grow on your head like those of the devil. Like the devil, you are misleading people.

In case 28 of *The Book of Equanimity*, a monk says to Gokoku, "When a crane stands on a withered pine, then what?"

Gokoku said, "On the ground below, it's a shame."

As we've seen, the withered pine represents the state of emptiness. Master Tozan once said, "The spirit tree is sublime, but the crane doesn't stay there."[5] The monk thinks he's realized something. But Tozan reminds us that the crane doesn't stay there.

In his comments on this case, Master Wanshi Bansho said, "This monk took this little bit of scenery and stuck it on his forehead, showing it to everyone he met." The monk was saying, "Look at me! I've realized something!" Gokoku's reply is basically saying, "I'm standing down here on the ground, and you're up on this lofty place. From my position, your position looks like a real shame."

Even if you have some kind of opening or a glimpse of that empty state, if you attach to it, and the view of self still persists, you plummet into the ice cave. That is a Zen sickness. This view of self keeps raising its horns, and you have to be on constant watch. Maezumi Roshi used to say, "Practice is about serving without being noticed." We serve without any expectation of return, recognition, or merit.

In this drifting, wandering world, it is very difficult to cut off attachments—to not rear up the head's horn even a little. When we reflect on our vows, we are vowing to let attachments go and realize the truth of emptiness. This is an expression of true gratitude.

In case 38 of *The Book of Equanimity*, Rinzai addressed the assembly, saying, "There is a true person of no rank. He is always leaving and entering the gates of your face. You beginners who have not witnessed him: Look! Look!"

No rank is "no basis on which to depend," a phrase from case 37 of *The Book of Equanimity*. You can't pull your rank: "Because I'm the boss, I said so!" "Because I am your mother, I said so!" "Because I'm the clown, I get to act this way!" No rank means to strip away all of your credentials and see who you truly are beyond all labels, ideas, and stories.

It doesn't take long to investigate all the credentials that we have accumulated to define who we are and to make ourselves better than or distinctive from others. We have our relationships. We are daughters, sons, mothers, fathers, sisters, and brothers. If we are really special, we are grandparents or the teacher's pet.

What about our work? I am an architect. Or I am a teacher, computer programmer, dancer, or social worker. I am rich. I help others to live healthier and more productive lives. I am an accomplished military officer, and I have the epaulets on my shoulders and ribbons and medals on my chest to prove it. I am a college graduate with an advanced degree. I am a Zen master.

What would it be like if we were able to forget these identifications? Can you go even further and let go of your identity of being male, female, or another gender? How about old, young, healthy, ill, tall, or short?

Attachment to credentials is very sneaky. The Buddha discovered this when he renounced his kingdom and tried to become an ascetic. Being an ascetic, which he perfected, became a credential. He discovered there was no lightheartedness or humor in the achievement. So, having tried the extremes of royal indulgence and yogic renunciation, he finally gave up. Under the Bodhi tree, he discovered the Middle Way, a true path and practice that anyone could follow, whether Brahmin or untouchable, male or female or other.

As I mentioned in chapter 4, when Yakusan was challenged by one of his students about why he did things a certain way, he said, "I am limping and palsied, ungainly in a hundred ways, clumsy in a thousand. Yet I go on this way." This reminds me of a story about Maezumi Roshi. He was sitting on the front porch at the Zen Center in Los Angeles when a drunkard came off the street, sat next to him, and said, "How is it to be enlightened?" Roshi said, "Very depressing."[6]

Near the end of his life, Master Joshu said, "Originally I intended to practice to help save others. Who would have suspected that instead I would become an idiot?"[7] In this rank, there is no self and no others. So, Joshu facetiously calls himself an idiot because he goes on saving others.

Yakusan is clumsy, and Joshu is an idiot. Which is the true person of Zen? Where does that source of knowledge not reach? Master Wanshi wrote this verse, "Throughout the Dharma realm all becomes his food." (*The Book of Equanimity*, case 69) Having no preferences, you can eat everything and be enlightened by everything. You can liberate everyone, even those with horns.

Don't even have a trace of self-importance. It is a disgrace to hang on to any achievement. The slightest bit extra on top of your head is a blemish.

A mind set on the quest of Buddhahood is shameful indeed!

Maezumi Roshi said, "Don't seek enlightenment," and, "Don't think that enlightenment does not exist." It is a shame to use one's meditation practice to seek fame or profit. There are always struggles for position and influence within sanghas, as within any human groups. It can take all kinds of shapes and forms.

When I went to the Zen Center of Los Angeles, I felt that I could do things better than anyone else there. I was a great manager and organizer. But Maezumi Roshi and Bernie Glassman declined to give me important positions, and I felt they were holding me down. Then I realized that I just wanted to spend my days sitting zazen and pulling weeds in the garden. When I realized that, they gave me important positions, and I was disappointed. I had to start serving like Yakusan—palsied and limping. With position comes responsibility and, sometimes, abuse from others.

The slightest thought of superiority is a shame. The slightest thought of enlightenment is a shame.

The same monk who asked about a crane standing on a withered tree asked Gokoku, "When dripping water freezes, what then?"

Gokoku replied, "After sunrise, it's a shame." (*Book of Equanimity*, case 28)

The monk is claiming that he has cut off all thoughts, feelings, and activities in his quest for Buddhahood. What good does that do? When the sun comes out, the water will thaw, and there you will be again in the midst of your busy life with all of its demands, complications, and chaos. Then what?

Even though there are no "others," nevertheless, it is a shame to ignore all the other people who cry out for relief from their suffering. A life focused on one's own liberation without any consideration of others is shameful indeed.

The far distant empty eon [kalpa]—no one has known it yet.

A kalpa is a vast amount of time, but in Buddhist mythology, there are four of them: the empty kalpa, the kalpa of growth, the kalpa of dwelling, and the kalpa of decay. Buddhist philosophy describes the nature of thoughts in the same way. They arise, or grow; they persist, or dwell; and then they decay.

After the kalpa of decay, there's the empty kalpa once again. Nansen remarked, "I always tell others to receive directly, even before the empty kalpa." (*Book of Equanimity*, case 23) Even though you intellectually understand it and can explain it thoroughly, it does not compare to personally experiencing it once. Even before a thought arises, see directly. Thoughts continually arise, but when you pay close attention, you will be able to perceive the gaps between thoughts.

You should be able to feel a thought arising with your whole body. Just as your body adjusts without thinking when you ride a bicycle, your body can feel a thought even before it bursts into your consciousness. You do not need to engage it. If you don't engage it, it will disappear on its own.

According to the case of the Fourteenth Ancestor in *The Transmission of Light*, when Kabimora Sonja was received by the naga king, he was given a wish-fulfilling pearl. Nagarjuna asked him, "This pearl is the most valuable pearl in the world. Is it form or nonform?"

Sonja said, "You only know about it being form or nonform. You do not know that this pearl is neither form nor nonform. Still more, you don't know that this pearl is not a pearl."

Hearing this, Nagarjuna was deeply enlightened.

Kabimora Sonja pointed out that, bottom line, just because we give things names doesn't mean we know exactly what they are. The far distant, empty kalpa is so remote from any of our experience, it is no wonder that no one has known it yet. But a pearl or a jewel—we think we know what that is. If you were asked, what would you say?

In case 91 of *The Book of Equanimity*, Nansen pointed to a peony and said, "People nowadays see this flower as if in a dream." Who really knows what this flower is? In a dream we think it is real, but when we awake, we are not sure. Is it a flower, or is it not a flower? No one has known it yet.

I am reminded of a story about Chuang Tzu (Zhuangzi), the Chinese Daoist, who dreamed he was a butterfly.[8] When he awoke, he was not sure if he was a butterfly dreaming that he was man or a man dreaming that he was a butterfly.

Prior to thinking about who you are, who are you?

The Sixth Ancestor asked, "Prior to thinking good and evil, what is your original face?"

The self that is prior to the empty kalpa is another way to express Buddha Nature. When not a thought has arisen, that is the empty kalpa. What is there prior to the empty kalpa? No one has known it yet.

Zen Master Wanshi Shogaku said, "Do not be bounded by or settle into any place. Then the plough will break open the ground in the field of the empty kalpa. Proceeding in this manner, each event will be unobscured, each realm will appear complete."[9]

This vast limitless life, I don't know it; you don't know it. If we think we can define it, it is no longer vast and limitless.

What is the mind of not-knowing? For a person who strives to control everything around them, it is very scary to not know. But what do you really know?

How necessary is it to journey south to visit fifty-three sages?

This line refers to the pilgrimage of Sudhana, as recounted in the Flower Garland (Avatamsaka) Sutra.[10] Sudhana was a youth from India who was seeking *bodhi* (enlightenment). At the behest of the bodhisattva Manjushri, Sudhana took a pilgrimage on his quest for enlightenment and studied under fifty-three "good friends," those who direct one toward the Way to Enlightenment.

He visited Avalokiteshvara and the future Buddha Maitreya, among others. The final master he visited was Samantabhadra, who taught Sudhana that wisdom only exists for the sake of putting it into practice. It is only good insofar as it benefits all living beings. This is our bodhisattva vow manifesting yet again.

Do you know what he discovered? This very body is the body of Buddha. Wherever I go, I am there. It is a journey that leads me back to where I started.

The commentary to the ten ox-herding pictures starts like this: "Why the search? The ox has never been missing from the beginning."[11] But we get confused and wander into a deep place filled with thick fog and tangled briars.

Years ago, my children showed me a comic book with a main character called the Silver Surfer. He was a Marvel superhero who could jump on his silver surfboard and travel to the farthest reaches of this universe and other universes at speeds faster than the speed of light.

In this particular comic book, the Silver Surfer was trying to find ultimate truth. He got on his silver surfboard and went through all kinds of adventures, not only on this plane of existence but on other planes and in other universes, always looking for the truth. After going through all these dimensions, he finally found it—and, would you believe it, he found it at the very place where he started. He found ultimate truth under his own feet. That little comic book episode reminded me of Sudhana journeying south to visit fifty-three sages.

Our Zen journey is simple and straightforward, but it is not easy. First you have to find a good teacher and train. Then you must honor your teacher. Here is a story that conveys how Maezumi Roshi explained to me how to honor your teacher. About fifty years ago, I spent some time in Japan at Maezumi Roshi's family temple in Tokyo. His father, Baian Hakujun, was a dignitary in the Soto Zen school, and most of his brothers were Zen priests. They took very good care of me while I was there. When I returned, I asked Maezumi Roshi how to repay their kindness. He said you can honor them by diligently practicing zazen and realizing your true nature.

You don't have to run after anything or produce anything. You just need to let go of your cherished opinions. There is nowhere to go, and there is no teaching to grab on to. But this is only true after you have caught, tamed, and released the ox.

Yet you continue on your journey and with your practice. They have become an intimate part of you. So intimate that nothing is shared. That is what this fifth stage of the Kokun Goi represents. There is no duality. There are no others, so your life is not two. And there is no self, so it is not one either. Not one. Not two. Like Tozan said in the Fifth Hensho Goi: "Who can attune to that beyond what is and what is not?" What is beyond existence and nonexistence? The fifth rank of both the Hensho Goi and the Kokun Goi point to this state. It is like walking on the edge of a sword, falling to neither one side nor the other. That is Chu, the Middle Way.

There is not even a square inch of ground upon which to stand.

○　○　○　○　○

PRACTICE QUESTION

How necessary is it to journey south to visit fifty-three sages?

APPENDIX A

Hensho Goi and the Hexagrams of the I Ching

The Hensho Goi have been identified with different hexagrams from the I Ching (or Yi Jing), an ancient Chinese text that was used to foretell future events or discover hidden knowledge.[1] The hexagrams that provide that knowledge are formed by throwing coins or yarrow sticks.

Over the centuries, a considerable amount of commentary has pointed to the following hexagrams as corresponding to the Hensho Goi.[2] The specific hexagrams are alluded to in *The Song of the Jewel Mirror Samadhi*, which you will find in appendix C. The comments in this appendix are a distillation of the wisdom of the I Ching for the respective hexagrams, including my interpretations of how these hexagrams correspond to the Hensho Goi.

APPENDIX A

TRIGRAMS USED IN THE GOI HEXAGRAMS	CHINESE NAME	ENGLISH NAME
━━ ━━ ━ ━	*sun*	The gentle, wind
━ ━ ━━ ━━	*tui*	The joyous, lake
━━ ━ ━ ━━	*li*	The clinging, fire

HEXAGRAM	CORRESPONDING RANK	I CHING REFERENCE
━━ ━━ ━ ━ ━━ ━━ ━ ━	First Rank Relative in the midst of the absolute [double wind]	57. The Gentle (the penetrating, wind) It is the wind that disperses the clouds, leading to vast clear sky.
━ ━ ━━ ━━ ━ ━ ━━ ━━	Second Rank Absolute in the midst of the relative [double lake]	58. The Joyous, lake True joy rests in firmness and strength within while manifesting as yielding and gentle.

▬ ▬ ▬▬▬ ▬▬▬ ▬▬▬ ▬▬▬ ▬ ▬	Third Rank Coming in the midst of the absolute [lake above, wind below]	28. Preponderance of the Great Strong inside, weak outside. This condi- tion must pass or misfortune arises.
▬▬▬ ▬▬▬ ▬ ▬ ▬ ▬ ▬▬▬ ▬▬▬	Fourth Rank Reaching in the midst of the relative [wind above, lake below]	61. Inner Truth Wind blows over the lake. The vis- ible effects of the invisible manifest, indicating a heart free of prejudice and open to truth.
▬▬▬ ▬ ▬ ▬▬▬ ▬▬▬ ▬ ▬ ▬▬▬	Fifth Rank Arriving in the midst of absolute/rela- tive (unity attained) [double fire]	30. The Clinging, fire Fire has no definite form but clings to objects and is bright. Its nature is in its radiance.

THE RELATIVE IN THE MIDST OF THE ABSOLUTE

I Ching Entry 57: Subtle Penetrating (double wind)

There is enormous power associated with this hexagram. It is associated with gentle penetration to the core and find-ing the base from which things arise. This stage lets you acquire a place from which you can influence the world you live in. Penetrate to the core, find the hidden disorders, and awaken inner wisdom. Do not impose a solution. Adapt like the persuasive power of the wind. In nature, it is the wind that disperses the gathered clouds, leaving the sky clear and serene. In human life, it is penetrating clarity of judgment that thwarts all dark hidden motives.

The penetrating quality of the wind depends on its ceaselessness. Many beautiful landscapes have been formed by the wind carving shapes from the rock. Penetration produces gradual and inconspicuous effects through an influence that never lapses. Results of this kind are more complete and enduring. Like water constantly dripping on rock and causing it to erode, the constant wind penetrates every gap and crevice to reveal the inner nature.

THE ABSOLUTE IN THE MIDST OF THE RELATIVE

I Ching Entry 58: Opening, Joyous (double lake)

This hexagram is symbolized by the smiling lake, and its attribute is joyousness. True joy, therefore, rests in firmness and strength within while outwardly manifesting itself as yielding and gentleness. Joy must be based on steadfastness and spring from a clear sense of your true nature.

Express your true self. Make an offering, and you will succeed. The double lake reveals innate forms, since joy is a beacon in the world when it manifests as the joy of discovery. Inner self-reflection gives you the ability to express the spirit in the human community.

COMING IN THE MIDST OF THE ABSOLUTE

I Ching Entry 28: Great Pressure (lake above, wind below)

A great transition—this is a crucial time of passage. It is a moment of truth that requires you to step out of conventional ideas. You are alone and need to manifest no fear. This is a critical situation. The structure of your life is in danger, but there is a creative force at work in this breakdown. Do not listen to conventional thinking. This is a time of change that recharges experience with meaning and energy. The best answers will be intuitive and spontaneous, and they will flow naturally from the need.

REACHING IN THE MIDST OF THE RELATIVE

I Ching Entry 61: Centering in Truth (wind above, lake below)

Centering in truth involves finding the connection between your heart and the circumstances of your life. You will connect to your center and reveal the inner wisdom that penetrates you, all beings, and all dharmas. Let go of prejudices and be open-hearted to the truth of the world as it is. Connect your life to the spirit.

ARRIVING IN THE MIDST OF ABSOLUTE/RELATIVE (UNITY ATTAINED)

I Ching Entry 30: Radiance (double fire)

Fire is the symbol of liberation, but it needs fuel to burn. The ability to radiate love and light depends on our interconnections with others. Everything is related. Radiance is visionary. Let go of the past and brighten all that is hidden. Take care of your base, and it will take care of you. The ten thousand dharmas advance and realize the self.

APPENDIX B

Hensho Goi and the Five Wisdoms and the Five Buddha Energies

In this appendix, we look at the relationship between the Hensho Goi, the five wisdoms, and the five Buddha energies. It was Hakuin who first identified the relationship between the Hensho Goi and the Buddha Wisdoms.[1]

HENSHO GOI	WISDOM	BUDDHA ENERGY
1. The relative in the midst of the absolute	Mirror-like wisdom	*Vajra* (clarity)
2. The absolute in the midst of the relative	Universal nature wisdom or wisdom of equanimity	*Ratna* (creativity, richness)
3. Coming in the midst of the absolute	Marvelous observing or discriminating wisdom	*Padma* (passion)
4. Reaching in the midst of the relative	Perfection of action or all-accomplishing wisdom	*Karma* (activity)
5. Arriving in the midst of absolute/relative (unity attained)	Wisdom of all-pervading space	*Buddha* (spacious)

The relative in the midst of the absolute corresponds to the great perfect mirror wisdom or mirror-like wisdom, which is Vajra energy. This energy represents clarity and reflects what it sees without bias. When people manifest the wisdom aspect of Vajra, they are clear-minded with an intellectual brilliance, sharp and precise. They maintain a perspective and are full of integrity.

The absolute in the midst of the relative corresponds to the universal nature wisdom, or wisdom of equanimity, which is Ratna energy. This energy represents richness and creativity. The Ratna family exudes a golden yellow energy that encompasses and enriches everything. This energy displays equanimity and satisfaction. When people manifest the wisdom aspect of Ratna, they are expansive, creative, resourceful, hospitable, and appreciative.

Coming in the midst of the absolute corresponds to the marvelous observing wisdom, or discriminating wisdom, which is Padma energy. This energy represents passion. The Padma family glows with the vitality of red energy. The wholesome aspect of Padma energy is a finely tuned intuition that discriminates subtle experiences without bias. When people manifest the wisdom of Padma, they are engaging, magnetizing, and charming. This energy listens deeply and speaks from the heart.

Reaching in the midst of the relative corresponds to the perfection of action wisdom, or all-accomplishing wisdom, which is Karma energy. This energy is represented by activity. The Karma family emits a green energy, swift and energetic like the wind. Karma energy leads to all-accomplishing action for the benefit of others. When people exhibit the wholesomeness of Karma, they can be efficient, effective, and practical. Full of confident energy, they act in timely and appropriate ways in synchronicity with the world.

Arriving in the midst of absolute/relative (unity attained) corresponds to the wisdom of all-pervading space, which is Buddha energy. This energy is represented by spaciousness. Buddha energy is all-pervasive and peaceful. When people manifest the wisdom aspect of Buddha energy, they are receptive, accommodating, easygoing, and content with just being.

Each stage or rank contains all the other stages. The Five Ranks of the relative and absolute contain and build on each other. As your insight and understanding grow, you evolve through all of the ranks, wisdoms, and energies. You never end up at the same place you started.

If we consider the five Buddha energies, we can see how each energy appears in each stage and evolves with the new insight. At every juncture in our lives, it is important to have the clarity of Vajra energy to see the nature of our choices. Connecting with Ratna energy, we can be creative and resourceful in making those choices. Karma energy brings the insight to act appropriately, and Padma energy gives us the intuitive knowledge that we are moving in the right direction. Our Buddha energy holds it all together in peaceful space.

Intrinsically each of us is complete; there is nothing lacking and nothing extra. How to realize that state experientially is the big challenge.

APPENDIX C

The Song of the Jewel Mirror Samadhi

The Song of the Jewel Mirror Samadhi is reproduced here with my comments. Some pundits believe that the inspiration for the Five Ranks comes from this poem, which is attributed by some to Tozan. However, in *The Record of Tozan*, it says that he learned it from his teacher, Ungan Donjo, who learned it from his teacher, Yakusan Igen. It is part of the secret teaching transmitted from teacher to student. In this appendix, I reproduce the verse with my comments in brackets interspersed between the lines.

> The dharma of suchness is intimately transmitted
>   by buddhas and ancestors.
> [*Suchness is awakening to one's true self.*]

> Now you have it; preserve it well.
> [*If you don't see it, it doesn't matter if you have it.*]

> A silver bowl filled with snow, a heron hidden in
>   the moon.
> Apart they seem similar, together they are different.

*[Can you distinguish eggs from chicken poop? What about
gold from fool's gold?]*

The Mind, not resting in words, accommodates
what arises.
[Like the mirror.]

Move and you are trapped; miss and you fall into
doubt and vacillation.
Neither ignore nor confront it, for it is like a great
ball of fire.
*[Perfect wisdom is like a ball of flames; it can't be grasped
from any side.]*

Just to portray it in literary form is to stain it with
defilement.
[Words do not reach it.]

In darkest night it is perfectly clear; in the light of
dawn it is hidden.
*[See the first Hensho rank: we meet without knowing each
other.]*

It is a standard for all things; its use removes all
suffering.
Although it takes no action, it is not without words.
*[Dead words don't express it, but hearing live words you
should grasp the Great Reality.]*

Like facing a jeweled mirror; form and reflection
   behold each other.
[*See the second Hensho rank: the ignorant woman finds her
   ancient mirror.*]

You are not it, but in truth it is you.
[*What are you, other than it? It, in this instance, is the
   dharma of suchness.*]

Like a newborn child, it is fully endowed with five
   aspects:
No going, no coming, no arising, no abiding;
[*The five characteristics of an infant are analogous to those
   of the Buddha—ultimately he doesn't get up, stay put,
   come, go away, or talk. The Buddha does not abide in
   the Dharma. See the third Hensho rank: everything
   disappears into the absolute state.*]

Baba wawa—speaking without speaking
In the end it says nothing, for the words are not yet
   right.
[*If you don't understand it, you might as well chant the
   sutras into the ear of a horse. See the fourth Hensho
   rank: there is no need to avoid a conflict.*]

In the hexagram "double fire," phenomena and the
   real interact
[*The fifth Hensho rank is "double fire" [double li]. See the
   charts of hexagrams in appendix A.*]

Piled up they become three; the permutations make five.

[*As a mathematician, I say permutations of three are six, not five. But another translation of* permutations *is "transformations." You are the one that is transformed by the hexagrams.*]

Like the taste of the five-flavored herb, like the five-pronged vajra (diamond scepter).

Wondrously embraced within the real, drumming and singing begin together.

Penetrate to the root and you fathom the branches, embrace the territory, and treasure the roads.

[*See the fifth Hensho rank: unity is attained.*]

You would do well to respect this; do not neglect it.

Natural and wondrous, it is not a matter of delusion or enlightenment.

[*Again, see the fifth Hensho rank: beyond what is and what is not. The next few lines also refer to this rank.*]

Within causes and conditions, time and season, it is serene and illuminating.

So minute it enters where there is no gap, so vast it transcends dimension.

A hair's breadth deviation, and you are out of tune.

Now there are sudden and gradual, because teachings and approaches have been set up.

[*Refers to the two Zen schools of sudden enlightenment and gradual enlightenment.*]

With teachings and approaches distinguished, standards arise.
[*Do not judge by any standards.*]

Whether teachings and approaches are mastered or not, reality constantly flows.
[*Intrinsically there is always absolute reality, whether we realize it or not.*]

Outside still and inside trembling, like tethered colts or cowering rats.
The ancient sages having compassion for such people, made a gift of the Dharma.
[*Utilize the gift, and both inside and outside will become still.*]

Led by their inverted views, they take black for white.
When inverted thinking stops, the affirming mind naturally accords (is self-affirmed).
[*At this stage experience merges with the intrinsic truth.*]

If you want to follow in the ancient tracks, please consider the sages of the past.
One on the verge of realizing the Buddha Way contemplated under a tree for ten kalpas.

[*See* Gateless Gate, *case 9. A monk asked Master Seijo of Koyo, "Daitsu Chisho Buddha did zazen on a bodhi seat for ten kalpas. Buddha Dharma was not manifested, nor did he attain Buddhahood. Why was it?"*]

Like a battle-scarred tiger, like a horse with shanks gone grey.
[*If one persists, like the tiger and horse, one can realize the dharma of suchness.*]

For the benefit of those with inferior ability, there is a jeweled footrest and brocaded robes
[*Refers to the story of the prodigal son, who left his rich family and wandered around forgetting that he was wealthy, in the Lotus Sutra.*]

For the benefit of those capable of wonder, a wild cat and white oxen
[*In case 69 of* The Book of Equanimity, *Nansen said, "Buddhas and Ancestors do not know of it; cows and cats know of it."*]

With his archer's skill, Yi hit the mark at a hundred paces.
But when arrows meet head-on, how could it be a matter of skill?
[*When absolute and relative merge, no skill is involved. It is just a matter of letting go of attachments.*]

The wooden man starts to sing, the stone woman
gets up dancing.
It is not attained in thought or feelings, so how to
reflect on it?
[*This expresses how to be free from constraints.*]

Ministers serve their lords, children obey their
parents.
Not obeying is not filial, failure to serve is no help.
[*These lines reflect ancient Chinese society. What is our
duty? It also refers to relative and absolute.*]

Practicing unobserved, functioning secretly, like a
fool, like an idiot.
[*This is like the old ignorant woman finding her ancient
mirror; no trace remains.*]

Just to continue in this way is called the host within
the host.
[*"Host within the host" represents being awakened and
functioning completely from that awakened state; it continues forever.*]

APPENDIX D

Kokun Goi and the Ten Ox-Herding Pictures

The Zen ox-herding pictures,[1] or stages, represent the path to the discovery of our true self, which is depicted by the ox. The Kokun Goi also represent that path. This appendix briefly presents the ten ox-herding stages and compares them with the Kokun Goi.

SUMMARY OF THE TEN OX-HERDING PICTURES

Stage 1—Searching for the Ox

At this stage, you have your first genuine resolve to follow the Enlightened Way.

Stage 2—Finding the Traces of the Ox

In this stage, you have a cerebral understanding of the existence of the ox. Part of that understanding comes from your actual practice. As a result, your faith in practice grows, and you begin to believe that even you can realize your true self. Nevertheless, you still cannot distinguish between what is genuine and what is not, not to mention what is true and what is false. You cannot yet pass through the gateless gate.

Stage 3—Catching Sight of the Ox

At this third stage, you go further into the real origin of being and come upon the great way, which brings knowledge and insight into accord with one another. At this stage, most people get a glimpse of the ox but are not quite sure what they saw. With continual practice, the ghostly figure becomes clearer. When you open your eyes and take a look, you see nothing other than yourself.

Stage 4—Catching the Ox

At this stage of training, you see into the nature of the heart, right down to its fundamental source. However, this insight needs to be manifested in your life. Only when you take your hand away from the cliff, fall into the abyss, and having caught your breath, awake again—with astonishment—to life, do you catch the ox. Here is the place where you see into Buddha Nature and gain the infinitely great life of the cosmos.

Although you have seen into your original nature, it is still hard for you to always let the right thoughts persist. You have lived too long in the bushes of erroneous opinions and the dust of the intellect. Your ox is still wild and animallike, and it wants to pull you back by the reins into the world of habitual behavior to which you are accustomed. You are pleased when others praise and respect you, but if someone finds fault with you or slanders you, you get angry and bear a grudge. You have indeed caught the ox, but it has not yet come to be your real life. You still cannot know real freedom.

Stage 5—Taming the Ox

In the stage of taming the ox, everything that you have realized becomes an integral part of you. The training after the breakthrough begins, which consists of bringing the ox and yourself to one pure whole, in all coming and going and in all the circumstances of daily life. At the same time, taming means letting the self and being come to pure unity, in which the self sinks into being and vice versa. As the old masters say, it is extremely difficult to let this unity always persist. The breakthrough is usually sudden and instantaneous, but the training afterward—to allow what has been won to constantly persist—has to be gradual.

One Zen master said that post-satori practice is more difficult than pre-satori practice precisely because of the habit-ridden consciousness.

Stage 6—Riding the Ox Home

Now the struggle is over. Gain and loss have also disappeared into emptiness. You sink into the ox, and the ox into you, such that the heart of the ox, you, and the world are concentrated into one. There are no worries anymore. The great awakening is completed. Great peace reigns in the world. Singing and dancing are the voice of the Dharma.

Stage 7—Forgetting the Ox and the Person Remains

At the seventh stage, even unity is passed through and left behind. The experience of the truth that has been won is forgotten. Awakened, you are independent of everything. You are your own master between sky and earth. There is no duality in the Dharma. The portrayal of the ox has been only a temporary expedient—like a snare in which a hare is trapped, or a net in which a fish is caught.

Stage 8—Forgetting Both the Ox and the Person

When you succeed in reaching this point, the mirror of your heart shines clearly, and your nature opens wide and clear. You leave error behind and do not attach yourself to truth. You dwell neither in error nor in awakening. You are neither worldly nor holy. Do not linger where the Buddha dwells. Go quickly past the place where no buddha dwells. If you are no longer attached to either, what is innermost in you can no longer be seen into, not even by someone who has a thousand eyes.

This stage is *dharmakaya*—which literally means the "body of great order," or the "body of the Dharma." *Kaya* means "body." That body is the true nature of the Buddha, or in Zen terms, Buddha Nature. Buddha Nature is ineffable, which means it can't be expressed. If you try to express it, that's something other than dharmakaya. The dharmakaya is your true self that is beyond True Self. Don't substitute something else for it.

Stage 9—Returning to the Source

At this stage, you do not allow yourself to be tricked by the transitory and deceptive images of the world, and you do not stand in need of any further training. If you go further along the way of ascending and succeed in reaching the ground and origin, then the mountain is the mountain, the river is the river, the willow is green and the flower red, through and through. Complete awakening is like not-yet-awakening, in spite of the great fundamental difference.

This stage is *sambhogakaya*, which means the "body of delight." This refers to the bodies of the buddhas who dwell in paradise. It's sometimes described as the ecstasy of enlightenment. It's a nice body. This is the state of "just this."

Stage 10—Entering the Market with Open Hands

When you have brought the experience of truth to completion within yourself, you go into the world to liberate others. You visit the drinking places and fish stalls, as you please, to awaken the drunkards there to themselves.

Nirmanakaya, the "body of transformation," corresponds to this stage. It is the earthly body in which buddhas appear in order to teach and serve others. It is represented by Shakyamuni Buddha. And in this case, it is Hotei, the Laughing Buddha.

COMPARISON OF KOKUN GOI AND OX-HERDING PICTURES

KOKUN GOI	OX-HERDING PICTURES
1. Shift	1. Searching for the ox
2. Submission	2. Finding the traces of the ox 3. Catching sight of the ox
3. Awakening	4. Catching the ox 5. Taming the ox

KOKUN GOI	OX-HERDING PICTURES
4. Collective awakening	6. Riding the ox home
	7. Forgetting the Ox and Person remains
	8. Forgetting both the Ox and the Person
	9. Returning to the source
5. Absolute awakening	10. Entering the market with open hands

NOTES

PREFACE

1. Thomas Yuho Kirchner, *Entangling Vines* (Kyoto: Tenryiji Institute for Philosophy and Religion, 2004).

1. ASPECTS OF THE FIVE RANKS

1. William Blake, "Auguries of Innocence," chap. 2 in *Songs of Innocence and Songs of Experience* (CreateSpace Independent Publishing Platform, 2017).
2. Mark Siderits and Shoryu Katsura, *Nagarjuna's Middle Way* (Boston: Wisdom Publications, 2013).
3. Norman Waddell, *The Essential Teachings of Zen Master Hakuin* (Boston: Shambhala Publications, 2010), xviii.
4. Watson, *Zen Teachings of Master Lin-chi*, 68.
5. For a detailed description of the Three Tenets, see Bernie Glassman, "The Three Tenets of the Zen Peacemakers," *Lion's Roar*, June 25, 2017, www.lionsroar.com/taking-the-plunge-street-retreat/.
6. This quote from Rumi comes from his epic work *Maš̱navī-yi Ma'navī* (*Spiritual Couplets*).
7. Yisroel Baal Shem Tov, *850 Sayings of The Baal Shem Ṭov*, trans. Zevi Wineberg (Las Vegas: ind. pub., 2020), 27.
8. Ramana Maharshi, *Who Am I? (Nan Yar?): The Teachings of Sri Ramana Maharshi*, trans. T. M. P. Mahadevan (CreateSpace Independent Publishing Platform, 2016), 4.
9. Powell, *The Record of Tung-Shan*, 24–25.
10. Wick, *The Book of Equanimity*, case 49.
11. Powell, *The Record of Tung-Shan*, 63–65.
12. Cleary, *The Book of Serenity*, 206.

2. WHAT IS THE ABSOLUTE? WHAT IS THE RELATIVE?

1. Florence Caplow and Susan Moon, eds., *The Hidden Lamp Stories from Twenty-Five Centuries of Awakened Women* (Boston: Wisdom Publications, 2013), 37.
2. Version used by the Rochester Zen Center, www.rzc.org /library/zen-center-chants/affirming-faith-in-mind/.
3. Great Mountain Zen Center, "Identity of Relative and Absolute" in the Chant Book, n.d., www.gmzc.org/standard-liturgy.
4. Suzuki, *Essays in Zen Buddhism*, 24.
5. Sasaki et al., *A Man of Zen*, 46.
6. Thich Nhat Hanh, *Thich Nhat Hanh Quote Collective*, n.d., https://thichnhathanhquotecollective.com/2021/05/14/6678/.
7. Edward Conze, *Buddhist Thought in India* (Ann Arbor, MI: University of Michigan Press, 1967), 243.

3. FIRST HENSHO GOI

1. Miura and Sasaki, *Zen Dust*, 68.
2. Miura and Sasaki, 66.
3. Miura and Sasaki, 68.
4. Kirchner, *Entangling Vines*, case 28. This poem is included in the two hundred miscellaneous koans in the White Plum koan curriculum.
5. Luis W. Alvarez, *Alvarez: Adventures of a Physicist* (New York: Basic Books, 1987), 58.
6. Cleary, *The Book of Serenity*, 87.
7. Dogen, *Dogen's Shobogenzo Zuimonki* (Boston: Wisdom Publications, 2022), section 4–5.
8. Andy Ferguson, *Zen's Chinese Heritage: The Masters and Their Teachings* (Boston: Wisdom Publications, 2011), 282.
9. Wendy Egyoku Nakao, "Hold to the Center," *Tricycle Magazine*, Summer 2017, https://tricycle.org/magazine/hold-to-the -center/.
10. Carl Jung, *Contributions to Analytical Psychology* (Redditch, UK: Read Books, 2008), 193.
11. Jack Kornfield, *A Path With Heart* (New York: Bantam, 1993), 129.
12. Red Pine, trans., *The Lankavatara Sutra* (Berkeley, CA: Counterpoint, 2013), section LXI.

13. Osho, "Seeing Tozan," Osho Stories, November 18, 2015, https://oshostories.wordpress.com/2015/11/18/seeing-tozan.

4. SECOND HENSHO GOI

1. Enyadatta's story is told in the Surangama Sutra. The version related here derives from our ancestor Yasutani Roshi's telling of it, which can be found in Kapleau, *The Three Pillars of Zen*, 57–60.
2. Miura and Sasaki, *Zen Dust*, 69.
3. Zenju Earthlyn Manuel, *The Way of Tenderness* (Somerville, MA: Wisdom Publications, 2015), 6.
4. Carl Jung, "The Philosophical Tree," in *The Collected Works of C. G. Jung: Alchemical Studies*, trans. R. F. C. Hull (Princeton, NJ: Princeton University Press, 1983), 13:335.
5. Cleary, *The Book of Serenity*, 293.
6. Charles Chu and Charles Egan, *Clouds Thick, Whereabouts Unknown: Poems by Zen Monks of China* (New York: Columbia University Press, 2010), 202.
7. Miura and Sasaki, *Zen Dust*, 69.
8. Hakuin, "Song of Meditation (Zazen)," in *Manual of Zen Buddhism*, ed. Daisetz Teitaro Suzuki (New York: Grove Press, 1994), 151.
9. Miura and Sasaki, *Zen Dust*, 70.

5. THIRD HENSHO GOI

1. Price and Wong, *Diamond Sutra and the Sutra of Hui Neng*, 37.
2. Price and Wong, 57.
3. Price and Wong, 74.
4. Miscellaneous koans (unpublished), Great Mountain Zen Center.
5. This story of Bankei is all over the internet, but it is not in *The Record of Bankei*. It is used as a koan by the Pacific Zen Institute (www.pacificzen.org/library/category/audio/?taxonomy=pzi_archive_koan&term=bankeis-miracle).
6. Richard Bryan McDaniel and Albert Low, *Zen Masters of China: The First Step East* (New York: Tuttle, 2012), 142–43.
7. Francisco J. Varela, Evan Thompson, and Eleanor Rosch, *The Embodied Mind: Cognitive Science and the Human Experience* (Cambridge, MA: MIT Press, 1991), 60.

8. Varela et al., 231.
9. Schrödinger, *Mind and Matter*, 36.
10. Leighton and Okumura, *Dogen's Extensive Record*, 9:58.
11. Yoel Hoffman, *Japanese Death Poems: Written by Zen Monks and Haiku Poets on the Verge of Death* (Tokyo: Charles E. Tuttle, 1986), 108.

6. FOURTH HENSHO GOI

1. Robert Aitken, *Mind of Clover: Essays in Zen Buddhist Ethics* (San Francisco: North Point Press, 1984), 105.
2. This quote from Jesus is not found in the New Testament but in the Gnostic Gospels of Saint Thomas, which were found in the Nag Hammadi dig. See Pagels, *Beyond Belief*, 31.
3. Burton Watson, trans., *The Vimalakirti Sutra* (New York: Columbia University Press, 2000), 38.
4. Adapted from Daiun Sogaku Harada Roshi in Wendy Egyoku Nakao and Peter Eihei Nanfu Levitt, eds., "The White Plum Lineage Precept Koan Study" (unpublished manuscript, 2021), 45–47. The last paragraph before the endnote citation are Harada Roshi's words.
5. Cook, *How to Raise an Ox*, 43.
6. Thanissaro Bhikkhu, trans., *Crossing Over the Flood: Ogha-tarana Sutta*, www.dhammatalks.org/suttas/SN/SN1_1.html.
7. Adapted from Nelson Foster and Jack Shoemaker, eds., *The Roaring Stream: A New Zen Reader* (Hopewell, NJ: The Ecco Press, 1996), 72.
8. R. H. Blyth, *Zen and Zen Classics* (Tokyo: Hokuseido Press, 1964), 2:10.
9. Otsu, *The Ox and His Herdsman*, 19.
10. Ruth F. Sasaki, *The Record of Linji* (Honolulu: University of Hawai'i Press, 2009), 185.
11. Miura and Sasaki, *Zen Dust*, 71.

7. FIFTH HENSHO GOI

1. Miura and Sasaki, *Zen Dust*, 72.
2. Torei Enji, *The Discourse on the Inexhaustible Lamp of the Zen School*, trans. Yoko Okudo (Tokyo: Tuttle Publishing, 1996), 275.

3. Thomas Cleary, trans., *The Flower Ornament Scripture: A Translation of the Avatamsaka Sutra* (Boston: Shambhala Publications, 1993).

4. Otsu, *The Ox and His Herdsman*, 88.

5. Hesse, *Siddhartha*.

6. This quote is the Buddha's reply to Kisa Gotami, who wanted him to revive her dead son. He sent her on a journey to bring back a mustard seed from each family that had not experienced death. She came back empty-handed. The story can be found in Paul Carus, *The Gospel of Buddha* (Chicago: The Open Court Publishing Company, 1917), 210.

7. Leighton and Okumura, *Dogen's Extensive Record*, 5:355.

8. "Ebola Doctor to Grads: Enter the Suffering of Others," interview by Rachel Martin, May 17, 2015, on *Weekend Edition Sunday*, www.npr.org/2015/05/17/407447354/ebola-doctor-to -grads-enter-the-suffering-of-others.

9. Shunryu Suzuki, *To Shine One Corner of the World*, ed. David Chadwick (New York: Broadway Books 2001), 43.

10. Huston Smith, "Aldous Huxley—A Tribute," *Psychedelic Review* I, no. 3 (1964): 264.

11. Phantom59, "The Six Paramitas (Perfections)," *Dharma Wheel* (online forum), October 21, 2009, www.dharmawheel.net /viewtopic.php?t=514.

8. NEW PERSPECTIVES ON THE HENSHO GOI

1. Cleary, *The Book of Serenity*, 277–78.

PART THREE: THE FIVE RANKS OF THE SEQUENCE OF MERIT

1. Aitken, *The Morning Star*, 140.

9. FIRST KOKUN GOI

1. Otsu, *The Ox and His Herdsman*, 5.

2. Charlotte Joko Beck, *Nothing Special: Living Zen* (New York: HarperCollins, 1993), 168.

3. Elisabeth Kübler-Ross, *On Death and Dying* (Abingdon, UK: Routledge, 1969).

4. Kapleau, *The Three Pillars of Zen*, 215.

5. Soyen Shaku, "The Sutra of Forty-two Chapters," in *Sermons*

of a Buddhist Abbot: Addresses on Religious Subjects, trans. Daisetz Teitaro Suzuki (Chicago: The Open Court Publishing Company, 1906), 3–24.

6. Siksananda, *Sutra of the Past Vows of Earth Store Bodhisattva* (Ukiah, CA: Buddhist Text Translation Society, 2003), 164.

7. Zenkei Shibayama, *A Flower Does Not Talk: Zen Essays* (New York: Tuttle Publishing, 1970), 33.

8. Torei Enji, "Bodhisattva's Vow," in *Daily Zen Buddhist Sutras* (Sydney: Sydney Zen Center, 1992), https://sacred-texts.com /bud/zen/daily-ze.txt.

9. This Tagore quote seems to have been part of a speech.

10. SECOND KOKUN GOI

1. Nakao, "Hold to the Center."

2. T. W. Rhys Davids, trans., *Buddhist Birth Stories; or Jataka Tales* (London: Trübner & Co. 1880) 96.

3. Ilia Shinko Perez and Gerry Shishin Wick, *The Great Heart Way: How to Heal Your Life and Find Self-Fulfillment* (Boston: Wisdom Publications, 2006).

4. Stevens, *Three Zen Masters*, 13.

5. Stevens, 20.

6. Fatma Reda, "Voice of Freedom," *Orlando Sentinel*, January 3, 2005, www.orlandosentinel.com/2005/01/03/voice-of -freedom-349/.

7. Haskel, *Bankei Zen*, 49–50.

8. Torei Enji, "Bodhisattva's Vow."

9. Ferguson, *Zen's Chinese Heritage*, 127.

11. THIRD KOKUN GOI

1. Otsu, *The Ox and His Herdsman*, 11.

2. Cleary, *The Book of Serenity*, 64.

3. Stevens, *Three Zen Masters*, 10–11.

4. Chang Chung-yuan, *Original Teachings of Ch'an Buddhism* (New York: Random House, 1969), 200–208.

12. FOURTH KOKUN GOI

1. Shunryu Suzuki, *Zen Mind, Beginner's Mind* (Boston: Shambhala Publications, 2011), 44.

2. Yuho Yokoi, *Zen Master Dogen: An Introduction with Selected Writings* (New York: Weatherhill, 1990), 27.
3. Barbara Brown Taylor, *An Altar in the World: A Geography of Faith* (New York: HarperOne, 2010), 97.
4. Leighton and Okumura, *Dogen's Extensive Record*, discourse 64.
5. Leighton and Okumura, *Dogen's Extensive Record*.
6. Hakuin, "Song of Meditation (Zazen)."

13. FIFTH KOKUN GOI

1. Otsu, *The Ox and His Herdsman*, 23.
2. Dogen and Kosho Uchiyama, Thomas Wright (translator) *Refining Your Life From the Zen Kitchen to Enlightenment* (New York: Weatherhill, 1983), 42–43.
3. Shibayama, *Zen Comments on the Mumonkan*, comments for case 1.
4. Cleary, *The Book of Serenity*, 291.
5. Cleary, 121.
6. Sean Murphy, *One Bird, One Stone* (Newburyport, MA: Hampton Roads Publishing, 2013), 71.
7. Cleary and Cleary, *The Blue Cliff Record*, 272.
8. Martin Palmer, *The Book of Chuang Tzu* (London: Penguin Classics, 2007), 20.
9. Taigen Dan Leighton, *Cultivating the Empty Field: The Silent Illumination of Zen Buddhist Master Hongzhi* (New York: Tuttle Publishing, 2000), 32.
10. Cleary, *The Flower Ornament Scripture*, chap. 39.
11. Otsu, *The Ox and His Herdsman*, 6.

APPENDIX A

1. Wilhelm and Baynes, *The I Ching*.
2. Powell, *The Record of Tung-shan*, 88n181.

APPENDIX B

1. Norman Waddell, *Poison Blossoms from a Thicket of Thorns* (Berkeley, CA: Counterpoint Press, 2014), 101–13. See also Rockwell, *The Five Wisdom Energies*.

APPENDIX D

1. For a more thorough discussion of the ox-herding pictures, see Otsu, *The Ox and His Herdsman*; and Loori, *Path of Enlightenment*. There are many different versions of the actual pictures. You can view some of them here: https://en.wikipedia.org/wiki/Ten_Bulls; https://tricycle.org/magazine/ten-oxherding-pictures/; and http://webspace.ship.edu/cgboer/ox.html.

SELECTED BIBLIOGRAPHY

Aitken, Robert. *The Morning Star: New and Selected Zen Writings.*
Berkeley, CA: Shoemaker and Hoard, 2003.

Cleary, Thomas, trans. *The Book of Serenity.* Hudson, NY: Lindisfarne
Press, 1990.

———. *Secrets of the Blue Cliff Record: Zen Comments by Hakuin and
Tenkei.* Boston: Shambhala Publications, 2000.

———. *Transmission of Light.* Boston: Shambhala Publications, 1990.

Cleary, Thomas, and J. C. Cleary, trans. *The Blue Cliff Record.* Boston:
Shambhala Publications, 1977.

Cook, Francis Dojun. *How to Raise an Ox: Zen Practice as Taught in
Master Dogen's Shobogenzo.* Boston: Wisdom Publications, 2002.

———, trans. *The Record of Transmitting the Light: Zen Master Keizan's
Denkoroku.* Los Angeles: Center Publications, 1991.

Dogen, Eihei. *Dogen's Shobogenzo Zuimonki.* Translated by Shohaku
Okumura. Boston: Wisdom Publications, 2022.

———. *Moon in a Dewdrop: Writings of Zen Master Dogen.* Edited by
Kazuaki Tanahashi. San Francisco: North Point Press, 1995.

———. *Shobogenzo.* 4 vols. Translated by Kosen Nishiyama and
John Stevens. Sensai, Japan: Daihokkaikaku, 1975.

Hakuin Ekaku. *Wild Ivy: The Spiritual Autobiography of Zen Master
Hakuin.* Translated by Norman Waddell. Boston: Shambhala
Publications, 2001.

Haskel, Peter, trans. *Bankei Zen: Translations from the Record of Bankei.*
New York: Grove Weidenfeld, 1984.

Hesse, Hermann. *Siddhartha.* New York: Bantam Classics, 1982.

Kapleau, Philip. *The Three Pillars of Zen.* Boston: Beacon Press, 1965.

Kirchner, Thomas Yuho, trans. *Entangling Vines: Zen Koans of the
Shumon Kattoshu.* Kyoto, Japan: Tenryu-ji Institute for Philosophy and Religion, 2004.

Leighton, Taigen Dan. *Just This Is It: Dongshan and the Practice of Suchness*. Boston: Shambhala Publications, 2015.

Leighton, Taigen Dan, and Shohaku Okumura, trans. *Dogen's Extensive Record: A Translation of Eihei Koroju*. Edited by Taigen Dan Leighton. Boston: Wisdom Publications, 2004.

Loori, John Daido. *Path of Enlightenment: Stages in a Spiritual Journey*. Mt. Tremper, NY: Dharma Communications Press, 1999.

Luk, Charles (Lu K'uan Yü). *Ch'an and Zen Teaching*. Vol. 2. York Beach, ME: Samuel Weiser, Inc., 1993.

Maezumi, Hakuyu Taizan. *The Way of Everyday Life: Zen Master Dogen's Genjokoan*. Los Angeles: Center Publications, 1978.

Miura, Isshū, and Ruth Fuller Sasaki. *Zen Dust: The History of the Koan and Koan Study in Rinzai (Linji) Zen*. Melbourne: Quirin Press, 2015. [An abridged version is available as *The Zen Koan*. New York: Harcourt, Brace and World, 1965.]

Nishijima, Gudo, and Chodo Cross, trans. *Master Dogen's Shobogenzo*. Woods Hole, MA: Windbell Publications, 1994.

Otsu, D. R. *The Ox and His Herdsman: A Chinese Zen Text*. Translated by M. H. Trevor. Tokyo: The Hokuseido Press, 1969.

Pagels, Elaine. *Beyond Belief: The Secret Gospel of Thomas*. New York: Random House, 2003.

Powell, William F., trans. *The Record of Tung-shan*. Honolulu: University of Hawai'i Press, 1986.

Price, A. F., and Wong Mou-Lam, trans. *The Diamond Sutra and the Sutra of Hui Neng*. Berkeley, CA: Shambhala Publications, 1969.

Rockwell, Irini. *The Five Wisdom Energies*. Boston: Shambhala Publications, 2002.

Sasaki, Ruth Fuller, Yoshitaka Iriya, and Dana R. Fraser, trans. *A Man of Zen: The Recorded Sayings of Layman P'Ang*. New York: Weatherhill, 1989.

Schrödinger, Erwin. *Mind and Matter*. Cambridge, UK: Cambridge University Press, 1958.

Sekida, Katsuki, trans. *Two Zen Classics: Mumonkan & Hekiganroku*. New York: Weatherhill, 1977.

Shibayama, Zenkei. *Zen Comments on the Mumonkan*. New York: Harper & Row, 1974.

Stevens, John. *Three Zen Masters: Ikkyu, Hakuin, Ryokan*. Tokyo, New York, London: Kodansha International, 1993.

Suzuki, D. T. *Essays in Zen Buddhism—First Series*. New York: Grove Press, 1994.

Watson, Burton, trans. *The Zen Teachings of Master Lin-Chi*. Boston: Shambhala Publications, 1993.

Wick, Gerry Shishin. *The Book of Equanimity: Illuminating Classic Zen Koans*. Boston: Wisdom Publications, 2005.

Wilhelm, Richard, and Cary F. Baynes. *The I Ching*. Princeton, NJ: Princeton University Press 1997.

Yamada, Koun. *The Gateless Gate: The Classic Book of Zen Koans*. Los Angeles: Center Publications, 1979.

INDEX

absolute reality, 5, 20, 107, 145,
    152, 269
    attachment to, 34, 38
    challenges in realizing, 28
    as experience, 30, 31–33
    experiencing and expressing,
        distinction in, 24
    in fifth Hensho Goi, 139–40,
        156–57
    Five Ranks and, 4–5
    freedom of, 33–34, 41
    glimpsing, 6, 20, 38
    identity of, 43–44
    and relative, comingling, 10,
        69, 123, 233–34, 270
    and relative, relationship of,
        34–39, 271
    and relative, separating,
        16–17
    in second Hensho Goi, 12, 50,
        69, 81, 148, 154, 255–56
    synonyms for, 29
    in third Hensho Goi, 85, 149,
        154–55
achievement, going beyond,
    238–40, 247
Aitken, Robert, 5, 136, 161, 190.
    See also *Morning Star*
all-accomplishing wisdom. *See*
    perfection of action wisdom
Alvarez, Luis, 52–53
Amida sutra, 22
Ananda, 207–8, 209

attachment, 76, 193, 194, 212
    absence of, 93
    to absolute, 34, 38
    to credentials, 246
    difficulty of cutting, 244–45
    end of, 276
    falling away of, 195–96, 217
    in fourth Hensho Goi, 155
    letting go of, 184, 203, 270
    to right and wrong, 126
    to self/ego, 19, 44, 61, 184
attainment, 119, 198, 221, 222–23
attention, 113–14, 139–40, 168–69
Avalokiteshvara, 251
awakening, 129
    collective, 220–26
    commitment to, 106
    ego and, 63–64
    functioning from, 271
    struggle as opportunity for, 54
    of third Kokun Goi, 202, 213
    as what is, 127
    See also kensho
awareness, 92, 112, 123, 130–31,
    153, 188, 230

Baal Shem Tov, 17
Bankei, 90, 194–96, 281n5 (chap. 5)
Baso, 93–94, 229, 230
Beck, Charlotte Joko, 190, 242
Beethoven; Ninth Symphony, 128
beginner's mind, 75
beliefs and opinions, 233
    letting go of, 80, 87–88

CREDITS

We gratefully acknowledge the permissions given to reprint the following material:

Robert Aitken, Goi poem translations from *The Morning Star: New and Selected Writings* © 2003 by Robert Aitken, reprinted with the permission of The Permissions Company, LLC on behalf of Counterpoint Press, counterpointpress.com.

Isshū Miura and Ruth Fuller Sasaki, material from *Zen Dust* by *Zen Dust* © 2015 by Quinn Press, reprinted with permission of Quinn Press.

William F. Powell, excerpts from *The Record of Tung-shan* © 1986 by William F. Powell, reprinted with permission of The University of Hawai'i Press.

John Stevens, material from *Three Zen Masters* © 1993 by John Stevens, reprinted with permission.